WINSTON CHURCHILL

Also by Peter Caddick-Adams

WINSTON CHURCHILL

PETER CADDICK-ADAMS

Swift

SWIFT PRESS

First published in Great Britain by Swift Press 2024

1 3 5 7 9 8 6 4 2

Text design and typesetting by Tetragon, London
Printed and bound in Great Britain by CPI Group (UK) Ltd, Croydon CRO 4YY

A CIP catalogue record for this book is available from the British Library

ISBN: 9781800753556
eISBN: 9781800753563

CONTENTS

FOREWORD

O VER twenty-seven years ago I entered the chamber of the House of Commons for the first time as a Member of Parliament. Full of elan and no doubt misguided confidence, I joined a small coterie of Conservative MPs who had survived the trenches against the Blair onslaught of May 1997 to sit on the subsequently heavily depopulated Opposition benches.

But the Commons is a great leveller. There will always be someone with more confidence than you and, more to the point, many someones with every reason to be. Thus it was, I am sure, a twenty-five-year-old Winston Leonard Spencer Churchill strode an identical route to park himself on the green benches after the 1900 general election more boldly than this thirty-four-year-old ninety-seven years later. This was, after all, the genesis of a political career which promised much and of which much was expected. As the *Church Family Newspaper* put it: 'Such a man as Winston Churchill must climb very high up the ladder of life. The world wants such men. They make history, they influence men's minds, they carry conviction.'

The layout of the chamber Churchill occupied has changed little, although it was completely rebuilt after the Luftwaffe rained terror on the Palace of Westminster, culminating in the firestorm of 10 May 1941. It is largely down to the force of nature which was Churchill himself. In October 1943 the then Prime Minister moved a motion which proposed setting up a select committee of the House to report on the rebuilding of the chamber and the damaged sections of the Commons. He was adamant it should be 'restored in all essentials to its old form, convenience and dignity'. After all, he contended: 'We shape our buildings and afterwards our buildings shape us.'

He insisted the shape continue to be oblong rather than semicircular, distrustful of the semicircular assembly, 'which appeals to political theorists, enables every individual or every group to move round the centre, adopting various shades of pink according as the weather changes'. Perhaps with more than a hint of conceit, let alone melodrama, he railed against logic, which, having

> created in so many countries semicircular assemblies which have buildings which give to every Member not only a seat to sit in but often a desk to write at, with a lid to bang, has proved fatal to Parliamentary Government as we know it here in its home and in the land of its birth.

Thus Churchill impressed upon the select committee, yet to be formed, a second condition: the chamber should be small and intimate, with no prospect of sufficient seating allocated to every member. He warned: 'If the House is big enough to contain all its members, nine-tenths of its debates will be conducted in the depressing atmosphere of an almost empty or half-empty Chamber. The essence of good House of Commons speaking is the conversational style, the facility for quick, informal interruptions and interchanges.'

Unsurprisingly, Churchill got his way. A select committee was formed under the Father of the House, Lord Winterton, who also held the distinction of once having been the 'Baby of the House', having been first elected at the age of twenty-one, even younger than Churchill. The select committee reported in January 1945. Churchill's 'brief' about size and shape was respected, and the new plan designed by architect Giles Gilbert Scott provided for 427 seats (give or take, depending on the size of respective members' posterior dimensions on the long benches) for the then 640 elected members. Clearance of the site began in May 1945, and the new chamber was officially opened in the presence of King George VI, on 26 October 1950.

As if the rebuilding being in the image so advocated by Churchill was not enough, colleagues were left in no doubt about the huge impression he made on the place when the arch connecting the Members' Lobby with the chamber became known as the 'Churchill Arch'. The original had been built by Sir Charles Barry following the rebuilding after the catastrophic fire of 1834. Churchill suggested the archway be rebuilt from the original damaged stonework, symbolising continuity, but also preserved as a 'Monument to the Ordeal' which the Palace of Westminster had been subjected to during the Blitz.

One thing the new boy Churchill was not confronted with when first taking his seat in 1900 was the larger-than-life bronze statue of himself designed by Oscar Nemon. It was placed on the vacant pedestal on the left-hand side of the arch in 1969, four years after the great man's death. Less still would he have been intimidated by the even larger bronze statue of Margaret Thatcher installed thirty-eight years later and which occupies the other side of the Members' Lobby. Both appear to dominate the rather less ostentatious bronzes of Lloyd George and Attlee, which complete the pedestal quartet in the lobby.

There is a tradition that former Prime Ministers do not qualify for a full-size statue until after their deaths. However, I remember well being in attendance for the unveiling of the Thatcher pointy bronze by sculptor Antony Dufort in February 2007, six years before her death. Standing behind the great lady herself, I heard her declare: 'I might have preferred iron, but bronze will do. It won't rust.'

Today there is a sign at the base of the Churchill statue exhorting visitors to refrain from touching. The reason – toe damage. Visitors, along with a few members, have traditionally rubbed the foot of their favourite statue on entering the chamber, for good luck. Such was his popularity that on more than one occasion the protruding left foot of the great man has had to be restored.

So, any new member coming into the House of Commons chamber cannot escape the huge influence Churchill has had on our workplace. Though it may now be almost sixty years after his death, you walk through his arch, under his gaze, and then you battle to secure one of the reduced number of seats on the benches in the intimate adversarial-style chamber he advocated. And if that isn't enough, being pointed at by

Mrs Thatcher on your way is a further reminder that you walk in the footsteps of parliamentary giants.

What on earth could you possibly say or do to match that? In his briefly interrupted parliamentary career between his maiden speech on 18 February 1901 and his retirement as an MP on 27 July 1964, over nine years after stepping down as Prime Minister, Churchill has no fewer than 29,232 entries recorded in *Hansard*, the Parliamentary record. This includes, of course, the famous, epoch-defining 'blood, toil, tears and sweat' and 'Democracy is the worst form of government except all those other forms which have been tried from time to time', masterpieces from the Dispatch Box. His lethally witty one-liners are difficult to equal. Take the description of his Labour opponent Clem Attlee as 'a modest man who has a good deal to be modest about'.

There are few places in the Palace of Westminster where Churchill doesn't feature. The Churchill Room, with its rather smaller but no less impressive bust overlooking diners, is one of the smarter function rooms, while in Westminster Hall his name is etched in brass for posterity. The inscription marks the spot where Churchill's coffin lay in state for three days, with over 320,000 members of the public filing past to pay their respects. As Edward Bacon in the *Illustrated London News* described them, they had the 'mesmeric effect of a river flowing past'.

Churchill was one of only three Prime Ministers accorded the honour of a state funeral, the others being Arthur Wellesley, 1st Duke of Wellington, and the Liberal veteran William Ewart Gladstone. While Wellington lay in state at the Royal Military Hospital, Chelsea, Gladstone and Churchill took centre stage in the huge Westminster Hall built by the son of the Conqueror, William II, and completed in 1097. It is a magnificent hall, at its genesis the largest building in Europe, and has survived the great fire of 1834, IRA bombs and the Blitz. From there Churchill's body was taken aboard a gun carriage to a state funeral at St Paul's Cathedral.

Westminster Hall is literally a place full of great history. By day it is bustling with visitors and staff going about their business as the main entry point to the Palace of Westminster. But by night, as I often take a detour after working late, when it is usually completely deserted, you really get a sense of the great figures of history who occupied the space in centuries past, dead and alive. Other than for Churchill and Gladstone, brass plaques also mark the locations of the catafalques where the late Queen lay in state, along with her parents and grandparents.

Recorded too is the spot where King Charles I was tried for treason and subsequently condemned to beheading in 1649. The same fate befell Henry VIII's Lord High Chancellor Thomas More in 1535, while the first governor general of Bengal, Warren Hastings, is one of the few to have stood trial in Westminster Hall and kept his head. I often take groups of visiting parliamentarians from around the world on tours of the Palace of Westminster, starting in Westminster Hall. Despite my best efforts to bring the great history of our workplace to life, waxing lyrical about the relevance of the Civil War, which led to a republic following the King's execution, or the break with Rome because of Henry VIII's libido, it is invariably the stop at the Churchill plaque which garners the most interest and name recognition.

His spirit is with us in the bars too. George Bernard Shaw's verdict on Parliament is also perhaps most fitting for Churchill himself: 'Alcohol is a very necessary article... It enables Parliament to do things at eleven at night that no sane person would do at eleven in the morning.' Hear, hear to that!

And, of course, well beyond Westminster, Churchill the politician is never far away. I remember being part of a parliamentary delegation to Iran in less turbulent times. We were entertained by the British ambassador at the imposing British residency in Tehran. There we were given dinner in the formal dining room, overlooked by a photograph of Churchill, Roosevelt and Stalin in the very same places where we sat, with little having changed about the decor. The original visitors' book attests to the occasion. The event was of course part of the historic Tehran Conference of November 1943, the first time the three leaders had met together, and at which they began to plot the closing stages of the Second World War.

Winston Churchill dominated British politics for much of the middle part of the twentieth century, but his reputation survives intact with later generations, as witnessed by his winning the popular vote as the Greatest Briton a few years ago. His domination may have extended on the world stage well beyond the British Isles, but as we are reminded every time we step into the Palace of Westminster, there was his natural stage. Those who come after cannot but be infected by the character he injected so forcefully into it. Proudly declaring himself a 'child of the House of Commons', he left behind a very proud mother.

TIM LOUGHTON MP

Tower of the Koutoubia Mosque

INTRODUCTION

A s a painting it is perfectly proportioned. In the centre lie the walls of Marrakech, their depth emphasised by left-sloping diagonal shadows, cast by the setting sun. The foreground is busy with tiny figures around the main gate, while the background is framed by the Atlas Mountains, whose snowy peaks reflect the Moroccan glare. The *Tower of the Koutoubia Mosque* – the picture's title – looms over the city; it is the hour when the muezzin is calling the faithful to prayer. Consisting mainly of whites, pinks and ochres, the image is a happy, confident one, conveying warmth with a sense of travel and exotic adventure. This portrait of Marrakech sums up its maker.

Expertly painted on 25 January 1943, the canvas speaks of antiquity and ritual, of far-off lands, emphasised by palm trees in the middle distance. Although he completed over 500 pictures, this was the only one made by Winston Churchill during the entire Second World War. In fact, the composition illustrates a refuge: a rare moment when we glimpse the war leader free from stress. It was also one of his best, and in 1948 he gifted it to President Truman with a note: 'This picture... is about as presentable as anything I can produce. It shows the beautiful panorama of the snow-capped Atlas Mountains in Marrakech. This is the view I persuaded your predecessor [Roosevelt] to see before he left North Africa after the Casablanca Conference.'

In addition to submitting canvases to the Royal Academy of Arts under the pseudonym David Winter – which resulted in his election as an Honorary Academician Extraordinary in 1948 – our subject was twice Prime Minister, holding the office for a total of eight years and 240 days. Sir Winston Leonard Spencer Churchill (1874–1965) has merited more biographies than all his predecessors and successors put together. It is tempting to see his career through many different lenses, for his achievements during a ninety-year lifetime spanning six monarchs encompassed so much more than politics, including painting.

The only British premier to take part in a cavalry charge under fire, he was also the first to possess an atomic weapon. Besides being known as an animal breeder, aristocrat, aviator, beekeeper, big-game hunter, bon viveur, bricklayer, broadcaster, connoisseur of fine wines and tobacco (apart from Pol Roger 1928 champagne, his preferred tipple was a Martini consisting of a glass of Plymouth gin and ice, 'supplemented with a nod toward France'), essayist, gambler, global traveller, horseman, journalist, landscape gardener, lepidopterist, monarchist, newspaper editor, Nobel Prize-winner, novelist, orchid-collector, parliamentarian, polo player, prison escapee, rose-grower, sailor, soldier, speechmaker, statesman, war correspondent, war hero, warlord and wit, one of his many lives was that of writer–historian.

Most of his long life revolved around words and his use of them. *Hansard* recorded 29,232 contributions made by Churchill in the Commons; he penned one novel and thirty non-fiction books, and published twenty-seven volumes of speeches in his lifetime, in addition to thousands of newspaper dispatches, book chapters and magazine articles. Historically, much understanding of his time is framed around the words he wrote about himself. 'Not only did Mr Churchill both get his war and run it: he also got in the first account of it,' was the verdict of one writer, which might be the wish of many successive public figures. Acknowledging his rhetorical powers, which set him apart from all other twentieth-century politicians, his patronymic has gravitated into the English language: 'Churchillian' resonates far beyond adherence to a set of policies, which is the narrow lot of most adjectival political surnames.

'I have frequently been made to eat my words. I have always found them a most nourishing diet,' Churchill once quipped at a dinner party; and, to paraphrase another Churchillian observation: 'History will be kind to me for I intend to write it.' Most of his long life revolved around words and his use of them: 'Churchill lived by phrase-making,' according to biographer Roy Jenkins, and certainly much understanding of his time is derived from the words he wrote about himself. Yet 'Winston' and 'Churchill' are the words of a conjuror, immediately conveying a romance, a spell, as well as wonder at one man achieving so much. It is an enduring magic, and difficult to penetrate. In 2002, by way of example, he was ranked first in a BBC poll of the *100 Greatest Britons* – among many similar accolades. A less well-known survey of modern British politicians and historians conducted by MORI and the University of Leeds in November 2004 placed Attlee above Churchill as the twentieth century's most successful Prime Minister in legislative terms – but he was still in second place of the twenty-one from Salisbury to Blair.

As much a global figure as a British politician, Churchill was one of the first international media celebrities. Something of a lifelong dandy, with his many uniforms (he was both an honorary colonel and an honorary air commodore) and hats, watch chains and walking canes, silk dressing gowns and siren suits, spotted bow ties and ever-present cigars, he was a man of props, which boosted his familiarity to people in the pre-television age. The cover of this book well illustrates the point. Winston never gave a television interview, but in 1954 he arranged a secret screen test with the BBC at Downing Street to evaluate the new communications medium (which he dismissed as a 'tuppenny-ha'penny Punch and Judy show') for himself. On viewing the grainy black-and-white footage, he decided it was not for him and ordered the film be destroyed. Though the screen test was recently rediscovered, it is through the medium of newsreels, wireless and his printed words that we associate his life.

The Churchill image has featured on postage stamps and coinage, with warships, tanks, locomotives, several schools, a Cambridge college, champagne, whisky, cocktails and cigars named after him. Blessed with intelligence, wit and wisdom, he was mostly self-educated, not having attended a university. (In later years he would sit as chancellor or rector of three universities and be awarded one honorary professorship and eleven honorary degrees.) Born in the era of boots and saddles, among Prime Ministers he was unique in being recommended for a Victoria Cross in his youth, and in old age in advocating the use of weapons of mass destruction. 'I want you to think very seriously over this question of poison gas,' he ordered his chiefs of staff on 6 July 1944, during the stalling Normandy campaign.

To retain a vestige of objectivity when faced with the Winston Spencer Churchill spell, modern scholarship is now concluding that his relationship with the historical truth was not always as objective as he himself would have us believe. David Cannadine has emphasised how aspects of Churchill's flawed decision-making and prejudices during the Second World War were played down or excluded from his account of the same name. Consider: in his six-volume account of the First World War, the Eastern Front gets a whole volume to itself, while in his *Second World War*, of equal length, the Germano-Russian war features hardly at all. New biographers have highlighted the importance of his many secretaries, personal aides and experts: it is not generally realised Churchill's major histories were written by teams of literary assistants and only polished by the putative author, who nevertheless minutely directed each enterprise. Author Sonia Purnell is one of the few to have highlighted the role of his strong-willed wife, Clementine 'Clemmie' Hozier (1885–1977), whom Winston married in 1908, but is referred to surprisingly little in his own works. Her rock solid but not uncritical support for him, particularly during the 'Wilderness Years' of the interwar period, her presiding over Chartwell, their country house in Kent, for forty years, and her prompts for him to show humility during the era of his triumph, shaped his character and policies, and shored him up during moments of depression.

We have John and Celia Lee to thank for reappraising the role of Winston's brother Jack (1880–1947), younger by six years, who was also airbrushed out of history, usually by Churchill himself. An engaging and honourable man who served in the South African Light Horse with his sibling, as a stockbroker he shielded his brother from the worst effects of the 1929 Wall Street Crash and lived in Downing Street during the war after being bombed out of his own home. The self-destructive behaviour of Winston's only son, Randolph (1911–68), also had a bearing on his father, who spoiled him. Churchill never referred to this, but during the 1930s, Randolph's affairs with the bottle and women, as well as his efforts to enter Parliament, caused rifts between his parents.

In the war years, Randolph's domestic disagreements with his parents grew so violent Clemmie thought her husband might suffer a seizure. Their son's erratic service with special forces behind enemy lines in Yugoslavia merely added to the Prime Minister's stress. Randolph would die in 1968, three years after his father, at the age of fifty-seven. Drink had turned him into a wreck, but Josh Ireland reminds us redemption of a kind was offered when, in 1960, Winston asked his heir to write his biography. During 1941, cast adrift and close to divorce, Randolph's first wife Pamela Digby (1920–97) conducted an affair with Averell Harriman, Roosevelt's special envoy to Europe, then coordinating the

Lend-Lease programme. Although this led to the breakdown of her marriage, according to Sonia Purnell (also a Digby biographer), her Harriman 'alliance' probably aided Britain's war effort significantly more than did the younger Churchill, and she supported Clementine as an energetic hostess at many important Prime Ministerial gatherings. Paradoxically, his daughter-in-law Pamela (who did eventually, after the death of her second husband in 1971, marry Averell Harriman) is considered far more important to the Winston Churchill story than his own son, Randolph.

The three surviving Churchill daughters (a fourth, Marigold, 1918–21, died aged two of septicaemia) also played important, supportive roles in his premiership, albeit ones which were minimised by their father, and left important memoirs. In the war years, each put on a different uniform of the women's forces, helping to project the Churchill 'brand'. The eldest, Diana (1909–63), served in the Women's Royal Naval Service (WRNS, known as the Wrens). Sarah (1914–82) worked in photo intelligence for the Women's Auxiliary Air Force (WAAF), accompanied her father to the Tehran and Yalta conferences and was romantically linked to the American ambassador, John Winant. Mary (1922–2014) joined the Auxiliary Territorial Service (ATS), commanded anti-aircraft batteries and travelled to Potsdam as her father's ADC. Although Winston and the formidable Clemmie enjoyed fifty-seven happy years together, their four children clocked up eight marriages between them. Winston's own personality swamped those of his family: they accepted he must come first – and 'second and third', in Clemmie's words – as he was so frequently away from home, 'either fighting wars or fighting elections', as Mary later observed. Thus, Churchill's wartime premiership was strongly underpinned by his extended family, though writers tend to be bedazzled by the man alone.

Modern Churchill scholarship, consisting of well over a thousand volumes, is an unrelenting tsunami, much of it still amounting to excessive hagiography, though now complemented by a growing school of iconoclasm which criticises Winston not only for his imperial attitudes, and for what he did or omitted to do, but also for what he claimed he had done in his books. The plenitude of primary sources makes his life as mammoth an undertaking for the historian as the two world wars with which he was intimately involved. To further confuse the enthusiast, there have also been to date sixty-three television and film portrayals of Winston Churchill, from cameos to full-on biopics, featuring fine actors from Albert Finney, Robert Hardy and Michael Gambon to Gary Oldman, Timothy Spall and Simon Ward. A good starting point for further study is the International Churchill Society, founded in 1968. It holds conferences, hosts podcasts, and publishes the quarterly *Finest Hour* magazine and a monthly e-newsletter, the Chartwell Bulletin.

In this volume on his premiership, you will find I have dwelled at length on Winston's earlier life, for the hinterland to 1940 explains how he acquired the personal tools to deliver a wartime Prime Ministership so effectively during 1940–45. He himself felt drawn not just to politics, but to the highest tier of governance, and often recorded a sense of destiny guiding his actions. Churchill truly believed he was destined for greatness, to the extent he saved everything he wrote. As a writer and biographer of his ancestor John Churchill, 1st Duke of Marlborough, and of Lord Randolph, his father, he was only too aware of the shortcomings of many libraries of personal documents, haphazardly collected like random archaeological sherds after the subject's death. Accordingly, he started his own. Many of the speeches, personal letters, newspaper reports and state papers cited here are the result of Winston's archiving of his own life, right down to household bills and receipts. These have ended up in the Churchill Archives Centre, Cambridge, established in 1973, which has also collected many other relevant papers, including those of Admiral Jackie Fisher, Brendan Bracken and Clement Attlee, and most have now been digitised. His life was recorded in print by his official biographers, son Randolph and, after his death, the academic Sir Martin Gilbert (1936–2015), in their immense, 3,111,090-word, eight-volume work, allegedly the longest in history, published between 1966 and 1988.

Accompanying it are the twenty-three exhaustive *Companion Volumes*, consisting of documents and papers, variously edited by Randolph Churchill, Gilbert and latterly the American scholar Larry Arnn, which appeared over the course of fifty years, from 1967 to 2019.* As the historian Lord (Andrew) Roberts reminds us, few other lives have ever been so minutely and comprehensively recorded through paperwork, which is one reason why so many volumes on Churchill have been penned. If you want to know about Winston's cigars, relationship with God or alcohol, culinary

---

* The twenty-three *Companion Volumes* stretch to nearly three *yards* and total an additional 15.3 million words.

tastes, war records, London tailor's bills or plans for painting holidays, then there will be documentation leading you to the appropriate subject, always accompanied by a sense the great man is looking down, nodding his head in approval.

PART I

Frustrated by the mobility of its Boer opponents in 1900, Britain raised a number of volunteer cavalry detachments. War correspondent Winston cabled back to London, 'More irregular corps are wanted. Are the gentlemen of England all fox-hunting?' He went on to serve in one of them, the South African Light Horse, under Colonel Julian 'Bungo' Byng, future field marshal and governor general of Canada. Here, Churchill wears a khaki tunic of his own design, bearing the single 'pip' of a second lieutenant, three medal ribbons, his Sam Browne (cross strap) over the wrong shoulder – and an impossibly rakish slouch hat, bearing Sakabulu tail feathers with the SALH clover-leaf badge on its left side.

CHAPTER 1

Frontiers and Wars

C HURCHILL'S parents influenced him in different ways. His mother was Jennie Jerome (1854–1921), daughter of a wealthy New York businessman and noted beauty, who had been introduced to her future husband by no less than the Prince of Wales (the future Edward VII) at Cowes Week in 1873. The pair were engaged three days later and wed at the British embassy in Paris on 15 April 1874. Winston was born at the end of the same year and John (Jack) in 1880. She was distant to her two sons during their childhoods in a not untypically Victorian way.

Her earliest letter to Winston's father, written in 1873, announced: 'I should like you to be as ambitious as you are clever... and I am sure you would accomplish great things.' After his early death, she switched her not inconsiderable powers of persuasion and allure to her elder son. Jennie married twice more after Randolph's passing, in 1900 and 1918, but remained devoted to the careers of her two boys. Winston later referred to his mother as his most 'ardent ally', acknowledging they 'worked together on equal terms, more like brother and sister, than mother and son', noting after her death she had 'left no wire unpulled, no stone unturned, no cutlet uncooked'.

Her strong-willed attributes were inherited by Winston, but the thread running through his life was the meteoric parliamentary career of his father, Lord Randolph Churchill (1849–95), whose twin-volume biographer he became in 1906. The second surviving son of the 7th Duke of Marlborough, whose appellation of 'Lord' was a courtesy title, Randolph had entered the House of Commons in 1874, in his mid-twenties, and quickly established himself as one of the leading figures in the Conservative Party, becoming both Chancellor of the Exchequer and Leader of the House aged thirty-seven. Most colleagues felt he was destined to lead the country, but within months he had fallen out with his Prime Minister, Lord Salisbury, and, in a fit of hubris, resigned from the Cabinet. Lord Randolph's political career was effectively over, though he remained an MP until his premature death.

In Winston's mind was not the tragedy of Lord Randolph's resignation letter of 1886, but of his passing nine years later, aged only forty-five. Obvious to Winston were his father's alienating mood swings, symptoms of vertigo, palpitations, mental decline and general inarticulation, and it was soon apparent a creeping illness was slowly robbing him of his persuasive powers in a very public fashion. This was later understood to be syphilis, a contemporary diagnosis believed by – among others – Winston Churchill all his life. As Lord Randolph's friend the future Prime Minister Lord Rosebery wrote: 'The progress of the disease was slow at first, but its signs were obvious, and when it began his career was closed... There was no curtain, no retirement, he died by inches in public.' While former Prime Minister and Churchill biographer Boris Johnson asserted Lord Randolph died 'in political isolation and syphilitic despair', modern medical analysis suggests a left-side brain tumour may more closely correspond to his known symptoms, a diagnosis supported by a host of biographers, including Robert Rhodes James and Richard Holmes.

The effects of this were threefold. First, Churchill was convinced he, too, might die young. He therefore became 'a young man in a hurry', determined to achieve as much as possible in the brief span he believed had been allotted to him. He also played up to this sense of impatience by stressing his premature birth, having been born to the seven-and-a-half-months-pregnant Lady Randolph on 30 November 1874. Second, believing his father to have been possessed of a sexually transmitted disease persuaded him to remain chaste to his wife, 'my darling Clemmie'. He never strayed and, indeed, they had a remarkably close marriage for fifty-seven years. Finally, Churchill – who lionised his father – felt Lord Randolph had been cut off in his prime, before he could go on to achieve greater things. Accordingly, the highest offices and a parliamentary career were expectations for the son, who lost his father when aged just twenty.

Winston later claimed he had had only 'three or four long intimate conversations' with his father, and spoke of his mother as shining for him 'like the Evening Star. I loved her dearly – but at a distance,' words which perhaps refer to Lord Randolph as well. The young Churchill thus had a very unusual start in life, inspired by both parents in different ways. Even had he wished it otherwise, history owned him from birth: he was born at Blenheim Palace, his Marlborough ancestor's mansion. Once described by the historian Simon Schama as a 'swaggering baroque pile,' the early eighteenth-century Blenheim is an important place to visit to understand the man.

Outside Parliament, much of Churchill's life revolved around big country houses: his own at Chartwell, the official Prime Ministerial residence at Chequers, and those of his relatives and friends. 'At Blenheim I took two very important decisions: to be born and to marry. I am content with the decision I took on both occasions,' he would assert later. After three unsuccessful proposals, he had re-encountered Clementine Hozier at a dinner party in London in 1908. Five months later, he invited her to Blenheim and proposed in a Greek-style lakeside summer house known as the Temple of Diana. Churchill would later pay homage to his ducal ancestor and the baroque palace created for him by Sir John Vanbrugh on behalf of a grateful nation, in his 779,000-word, four-volume biography, *Marlborough: His Life and Times* (1933–38).

On 16 November 1900 the correspondent of the *Church Family Newspaper* wrote of a public lecture given in London seventeen days earlier by 'a clean-shaved, fair-haired, pleasant-looking gentleman'. Introduced by the creator of Sherlock Holmes and personal friend, Arthur Conan Doyle (1859–1930),

> Churchill began his lecture in a modest, confident manner which at once riveted the attention of the audience which

crowded every part of St James's Hall [on London's Piccadilly]. For one hour and a half Winston Churchill played upon the audience with the skill of a master. He spoke without notes. He has all the gifts of an orator which spring over the footlights, all done without any apparent effort. In figure and movement, he is like his gifted father.

Winston, who in fact rehearsed his speeches fastidiously in order to appear effortless, was talking about his adventures in South Africa of earlier that year.

He had been brought up in the fashion of the day by Elizabeth Everest, a nanny engaged to attend to his early education, as his parents were lost in their own social whirl. Aged eight, Winston was dispatched to a harsh boarding school at Ascot, where his experience of caning echoed the worst of a Dickens novel, prompting transfer to a kindlier school in Brighton. Although Lord Randolph was an Old Etonian, he made an inspired choice in his selection of a different institution for his eldest son and heir. Two years after surviving a serious bout of double pneumonia, in 1888 the young Churchill arrived at Eton's rival, Harrow School in north London, where he disdained Classics but embraced History and English and got 'into my bones the essential structure of the ordinary British sentence – which is a noble thing'.

The Harrovian Army Class, hardly for scholars, prepared its boys for the muscular world of forces life. Entering the Sandhurst officer academy on his third attempt at its entrance examination, to the stricken Lord Randolph's fury, he was commissioned as a cornet of cavalry in December 1894, graduating a credible twentieth out of 130, just before the deaths of his father on 24 January 1895 (Churchill's own date of death exactly seventy years afterwards) and Mrs Everest, who passed away in the following July. This was the year he joined the 4th Queen's Own Hussars, a cavalry regiment of distinction dating from 1685. The loss of two people close to him initiated the 'young man in a hurry' syndrome. Then he heard of a war in Cuba, got leave, and dashed off in the autumn of 1895 to observe combat for the first time, spending his twenty-first birthday being shot at, something he recorded for the *Daily Graphic* newspaper.

This was the real reason for his journey to the troubled island. He had been left impecunious by his father (the term is relative in his case), and the *Graphic* promised five pounds an article. Churchill smelled excitement, and took ship, one senses, not least to test himself in someone else's war before embarking on his own. He was not disappointed. During one battle a nearby horse was hit, the bullet missing Winston by a few feet. Feeling destiny showing him his path, he discovered he had no fear of death, of close-quarter battle or of vigorously asserting his point of view. All were wonderful attributes to have discovered so young, and would stay with him for the rest of his days.

It was there he began another lifelong love affair – with Cuban cigars, on which he later opined:

> I suppose if I had to relive my life I ought to eschew the habit of smoking. Look at all the money I have wasted on tobacco. Think of it all invested and mounting up at

compound interest year after year... But consider! How can I tell that the soothing influence of tobacco upon my nervous system may not have enabled me to comport myself with calm and with courtesy in some awkward personal encounter or negotiation, or carried me serenely through some critical hours of anxious waiting? How can I tell that my temper would have been as sweet or my companionship as agreeable if I had abjured from my youth the goddess Nicotine?

The following year he was posted to Bangalore (today's Bengaluru) in India for nineteen months with his horsed cavalry regiment, and was housed like all young officers in a 'palatial bungalow, all pink and white... wreathed in purple bougainvillea, in two acres of land'. As a military cadet at Sandhurst, the young Churchill had come second in the equestrian exam, obligatory for all cavalry officers, and another test of his fearlessness. He found himself especially keen on polo and scored a hat-trick to win the inter-regimental cup for his team at Meerut in 1898. Winston's enthusiasm for the sport would continue long into later life, his last game played on Malta at the age of fifty-two, against Admiral Sir Roger Keyes. In addition to polo, Churchill embarked on a course of self-education, via an impressive range of academic volumes, from Plato's *Republic* and Gibbon's six-volume *Decline and Fall of the Roman Empire* to Adam Smith's *Wealth of Nations* and Macaulay's five-volume *History of England*. He collected butterflies, orchids and roses (other lifelong habits), read his father's parliamentary speeches in *Hansard*, and accompanied a punitive expedition against rebels in the Swat Valley, in the Khyber district of modern Pakistan.

Indian frontier campaigning was the world of Henry Newbolt's patriotic poem of 1897, 'Vitaï Lampada', with which Churchill was familiar, about a young man who progresses from public school cricketer to selfless officer of the empire:

> The Gatling's jammed and the Colonel dead,
> And the regiment blind with dust and smoke.
> The river of death has brimmed his banks,
> And England's far, and Honour a name,
> But the voice of a schoolboy rallies the ranks:
> 'Play up! play up! and play the game!'

It was also the era into which were born most of the young regular officers who would serve in the trenches of 1914–18 and become Churchill's generals of the Second World War. (Their descendants would go on to fight the offspring of the tribesmen opposing Churchill's hussars, in the British Army's last brush with the region's many frontier wars, during 2001–21.) The Swat expedition, under the splendidly named Sir Bindon Blood, led to Churchill's first book, *The Story of the Malakand Field Force* (1898), the result of the young officer's unique position of being allowed to write dispatches for the *Daily Telegraph* while wearing uniform on Blood's staff. The book does not disappoint, as this extract suggests:

> A single glass of champagne imparts a feeling of exhilaration. The nerves are braced, the imagination is agreeably stirred, the wits become more nimble. A bottle produces

a contrary effect. Excess causes a comatose insensibility. So it is with war, and the quality of both is best discovered by sipping.

As biographer Richard Holmes reminds us, Winston's secondment to the expedition was brought about by Jennie, his mother, but, as Blood conceded, his position was no sinecure: 'He is working away equal to two ordinary subalterns. He has been mentioned in dispatches already [for rescuing a wounded man under fire], and if he gets a chance will have the VC or a DSO.' Churchill's observation of those frontier days is best summed up in a single line from *Malakand*: 'Nothing in life is so exhilarating as to be shot at without result.' His immature novel, *Savrola*, inspired by his Cuban adventure, appeared at the same time, initially as a serial in *Macmillan's Magazine* from May to December 1898, then as a book in 1900, but was less well received.

Frontier campaigning was thirsty work and with Winston's choice of refreshment limited to 'tea, tepid water, tepid water with lime or tepid water with whisky', he sampled the last of these and discovered 'once one got the knack of it, the very repulsion from the flavour developed an attraction of its own... it was good for typhus and deadly on lice.' Churchill had not been a whisky fan at first. 'I disliked the flavour intensely,' he noted, recalling that Lord Randolph 'would never have drunk whisky except when shooting on a moor or in some very dull, chilly place'. Winston's frontier war changed everything and was the beginning of a lifelong affair, with a preference for Johnnie Walker – both the 'Black Label' and 'Red Label' varieties.

The rugged Swat valley was character-building, but Macaulay's *History*, whose author had been an earlier veteran of India, an MP and a Cabinet minister, was more influential in the long run in giving the slight, sandy-haired, rosy-cheeked young officer a sense of his country's history and his own place in it. Macaulay's flashy prose would find many an echo in Churchill's own works, with both sharing an understanding of the positive progress of British history, leading to a balanced governing constitution, forward-looking culture, and freedom of belief and expression, known in historiography as the Whig interpretation.

His *Malakand* book prompted a meeting with the Prime Minister, Salisbury, and attachment to General Sir Herbert Kitchener's military campaign in the Sudan. By then, Churchill was known as a medal-hunter, and it took a lobbying by his mother and Salisbury combined to overwhelm Kitchener's extreme reluctance (a scepticism which would hamper the Gallipoli landings of 1915 and endure until the general's death the following year). Again, Churchill secured a lucrative contract to write, this time for the *Morning Post*, contrary to all military norms of the day. Arriving in Egypt, he was attached to the 21st Lancers in Cairo and took part in the Battle of Omdurman (2 September 1898) – the British Army's last major cavalry charge with horse and lance. His book on the campaign, *The River War: An Historical Account of the Reconquest of the Sudan*, was published in November 1899.

At Omdurman his regiment had twenty-one killed, five of them officers like himself, with fifty men and 119 horses wounded, but this brush with danger did nothing to dent his self-confidence. He recorded the attack of a dervish warrior waving a fearsome bladed weapon: 'I raised my pistol and fired. So close were we that the pistol itself actually struck him. Man and sword disappeared below and behind me.' Churchill's charge might be taken as a metaphor for the way he lived, for he certainly reflected his life was like galloping at one's foes: 'So long as you are all right, firmly in your saddle, your horse in hand, and well-armed, lots of enemies will give you a wide berth.'

His Sudanese adventure also brought Churchill a wider understanding of the country's strategic importance to British interests in Africa, stretching from South Africa to Cairo, and of the real reason for Kitchener's presence – to keep out the French. He recognised too the region's bearing on Suez and the adjacent Red Sea, the midpoint of Britain's umbilical cord between London and India. Winston would never really shake the North African sand from his shoes. From the battles he ordered across the desert wastes of northern Egypt against the Italian and Germans in 1940–43 to his rendezvous with Roosevelt in Morocco in 1943, which resulted in the Marrakech painting, it was a corner of the globe to which he would be drawn throughout his life.

In his father's mould and destined, as he surmised, for politics, he resigned from the army but narrowly failed to be elected as MP for Oldham in a June 1899 by-election. Only Churchill – then aged twenty-four – could write of his first parliamentary defeat: 'I returned to London with those feelings of deflation which a bottle of champagne or even soda-water represents when it has been half emptied and left uncorked for a night.' Nevertheless, he did well enough for

Conservatives in the northern town, whose electorate was mostly employed in the local textile mills, to nominate him again to stand in the general election of October 1900.

Oldham was his first brush with the urban north of England, where his political antennae were initially guided by the cotton-spinners and their protectionist needs for taxes on cheap foreign textiles. For all of Churchill's fine living, the big houses, tailor's bills and general reluctance to identify with working-class life – he never rode on a bus, except to electioneer, or took a London Underground train, despite the otherwise splendid 2017 motion picture *Darkest Hour* suggesting he did – Oldham (at least in Winston's own mind) connected him with the working man.

Ever alive to international affairs – a trait which accompanied him throughout life – Churchill correctly foresaw the outbreak of the Second Boer War and arrived in South Africa in October 1899 as a well-paid war correspondent for both the *Daily Mail* and *Morning Post*, attended by his valet and a supply of alcohol including champagne, thirty-six bottles of wine, eighteen of aged Scotch and six of vintage brandy. Hunting for a story, two weeks later he accompanied an armoured train which was ambushed on 15 November. Churchill's leadership enabled the engine to escape, carrying the wounded to safety, but he was among twenty-three taken prisoner, with thirty-eight of the group killed and injured. His claim of civilian status as a journalist was ignored, and the aspiring politician went on to spend his twenty-fifth birthday as a prisoner of war in Pretoria.

On 12 December 1899, armed with a biscuit and four slabs of chocolate, he vaulted over his prison wall. Ironically, the Boers were already toying with the idea of his release. He also left behind two comrades who were supposed to accompany him. This became a pattern in his behaviour. It had to be him alone who succeeded or failed, rather like his father or John Churchill, 1st Duke of Marlborough. As well as luck and supreme self-confidence, there was a degree of selfishness, even ruthlessness in Churchill's psyche – hence the sidelining of his family in his memoirs.

By jumping freight trains and walking, he made his way to freedom 300 miles away. The story of his capture and breakout was the narrative of his November 1900 lecture in London, for instead of recounting the adventures of others, he now had his own larger-than-life tale to peddle. Churchill advertised his faith little, was only as familiar with his Bible as Harrow School required, and was not a regular church-goer, contrary to the norms of the day. Yet while on the run he encountered such physical and psychological lows he was forced to draw deep from the well of his beliefs in order to continue. He recorded how he 'found no comfort in any of the philosophical ideas which some men parade in their hours of ease and strength and safety. They seemed only fair-weather friends.'

Here he was partly alluding to, but not bemoaning, his own lack of university education, but he went on to communicate a rare insight into his soul. He surmised:

> No exercise of my own feeble wit and strength could save me from my enemies, and without the assistance of that High Power [God was often curiously omitted by name from Churchill's utterances or penmanship] which

interferes in the eternal sequence of causes and effects more often than we are always prone to admit, I could never succeed. I prayed long and earnestly for help and guidance. My prayer, as it seems to me, was swiftly and wonderfully answered.

This arrived in the form of John Howard, manager of a coal mine and the only Briton for miles around, who hid Churchill while the Boers looked for him, then loaded him onto a freight train to safety. After three days he crossed into Portuguese East Africa (today's Mozambique), and via the British consulate in Lourenço Marques (now Maputo), made his way by boat to Durban. With a Boer price on his head of £25 *dead or alive*, he found he had become an international celebrity, and for the first time in his life was fêted by a carnival of cheering crowds and rousing music.

After his escape, Churchill was reunited with his mother. She had raised £150,000 to furnish and equip a hospital ship, the *Maine*, and personally directed its medical activities. Winston also found, in Imperial Yeomanry uniform, his younger brother Jack, whom Jennie (about to become Mrs George Cornwallis-West, marrying a captain in the Scots Guards sixteen days older than Winston) was nursing on board after his wounding during the February Battle of the Tugela Heights, part of the campaign for the relief of Ladysmith. Alas, their three-day reunion was downplayed by Churchill in his captivating memoir, *My Early Life: A Roving Commission* (1930), on which the 1972 motion picture *Young Winston* was based. So too was the presence of his manservant, Thomas Walden, who had joined up with his master, but was left in camp on the day of Churchill's capture.

Equipped with a valet and a stash of fine booze, Winston's notion of campaigning was far removed from the rugged, ripping-yarn notion of man against the elements, implied by Baden-Powell in his 1908 *Scouting for Boys* and Churchill's own memoir. When Jennie and Jack sailed for England aboard the *Maine* with their cargo of casualties, Winston stayed behind, attached himself to the all-volunteer South African Light Horse and fought on, continuing to write at the same time.* He was recommended for a Victoria Cross by General Sir Ian Hamilton as a result of bravery at Diamond Hill on 12 June 1900, when another bullet clipped his headgear. However, his earlier claim to civilian status while a prisoner contributed to this being denied, as did antipathy from the War Office towards the 'pushy young adventurer'. As Churchill would later complain: 'I have many medals for adventure, but none for bravery.'

Later that year two books, *London to Ladysmith via Pretoria* and *Ian Hamilton's March* would appear from his hand about the campaign. Fine jacket artwork on the first edition of the former, published by Longmans, Green, depicted the ill-fated armoured train and both were copiously illustrated with maps and plans. They demonstrated the faith publishers had in Churchill's new-found bankability (never subsequently lost), and contain some of his best writing and most memorable turns of phrase. These, and

---

* Winston was extremely lucky in his commanding officer, Colonel Julian 'Bungo' Byng, future field marshal and governor general of Canada. They would aid each other's future careers.

lantern-slide lectures about his escapades delivered throughout Britain, helped secure his first entry into the Commons
as MP for Oldham in the general election of 26 September
to 24 October 1900.

Of the new member, full of confidence and promise, the
Church Family Newspaper's 16 November 1900 report exuded
prophecy, concluding with a remarkable final paragraph:

> One came away feeling how much we owed this young
> man, that one had been in the presence of a powerful
> personality – a personality gifted with a high intelligence,
> a fearless frankness, and the not uncommon power of
> looking at facts, and from those facts drawing original
> conclusions. Such a man as Winston Churchill must climb
> very high up the ladder of life. The world wants such
> men. They make history, they influence men's minds,
> they carry conviction because they are in earnest; and
> we, as Englishmen, may well feel proud to call Winston
> Churchill a countryman of our own.

CHAPTER 2

Gathering Storm

WITH his South African adventures still fresh in international memory, Churchill dashed off to the United States and Canada to deliver more talks, which netted him £10,000. While there he met President Theodore Roosevelt, and returned to make his maiden speech in the House of Commons on 18 February 1901. Thus, even as his parliamentary career began, in the minds of many, of which the *Church Family Newspaper*'s correspondent was but one, there was a uniquely heavy weight of expectation resting on the shoulders of this twenty-five-year-old man.

Winston Churchill had been gifted a sense of geopolitics, a world view granted to very few of his parliamentary contemporaries, who were steadily making their name working away at domestic issues. Before 1914, few would have visited North America (involving a week's passage by steamer), and though their university language skills may have suggested otherwise, many had not even set foot in Europe. For them Britain was the centre of an empire: by necessity, all matters should come to them; they should not have to venture out to enquire for themselves. Churchill, on the other hand, had no knowledge of the domestic lives of those he now had to help govern.

Instinctively, he discovered he was no imperial protectionist, which went down well neither with the good burghers of Oldham nor with his political party. Free from the 'philosophical ideas which some men parade in their hours of ease and strength and safety', Churchill again had to educate himself, and found himself more in sympathy with his Liberal opponents than with his own blimpish Conservative Party. Often found dining with bright minds outside politics, he would eventually, in 1911, co-found the 'Other Club', an invitation-only political dining society which met fortnightly at London's Savoy Hotel. Comprising politicians, lawyers, thinkers, writers, publishers, academics, educationalists and other members drawn from the top drawer of their professions, the club continues to meet, still to discuss, away from the straitjacket of party dogma, issues of the day. The freethinking conversations Churchill enjoyed at these and other early gatherings, his self-confidence and his wholesale adoption of free trade, against his party's adherence to protectionism, soon induced the young lion to cross the floor of the House of Commons and join the Liberals in May 1904.

Significantly, he sat in the place his father had occupied when, years earlier, Lord Randolph had been a rebellious young Tory in opposition. Churchill's move was extraordinarily fortunate, or perhaps prescient, for in the ensuing January 1906 general election the Conservatives were swept from power in a landslide defeat which saw the Liberals as the new party of government, winning 397 seats, with an absolute majority of 125. The new Independent Labour Party (founded in 1900) won twenty-nine, while the Conservatives' total of 156 MPs remains its worst result ever in a general election. Fought essentially over protectionism versus free trade, the election would have seen Churchill politically compromised and his political career over before it had begun, had he not jumped ship early.

Somehow, Winston also found time to pen a biography of his father during this period. Running to two volumes, the substantial 278,000-word *Lord Randolph Churchill*, written between 1903 and 1906, was well received, inspired his later *Marlborough*, and almost certainly was used by the son as a mirror to measure his own progress and his politics.

The incoming Liberal Prime Minister, Sir Henry Campbell-Bannerman, gave Churchill, still a relatively new face in the Commons, his first ministerial office as Undersecretary of State for the Colonies. This was on the strength of his rhetoric and force of character, rather than any residual family prestige. The Churchills were, after all, Tories. It was a high-risk strategy, notes biographer Roy Jenkins, as the Secretary of State, his political boss – the 9th Earl of Elgin (grandson of the sculpture-collector) – sat in the House of Lords, leaving Winston as the sole voice of the ministry in the Commons. His hard work brought membership of the Privy Council in 1907, permitting him the first of several post-nominal initials, 'PC', and the title 'Right Honourable'.

From July 1907 to January 1908, Churchill toured British East Africa and Egypt, exploiting his ministerial status to hunt big game. His boss, Lord Elgin, who resented his upstart junior, 'was not slow to applaud' his absence, it was said. The result was five travel articles eagerly snapped up by the *Strand Magazine* for £150 apiece, and a book, *My African Journey*, which netted him £500. When Campbell-Bannerman died in April (the only Prime Minister to die at 10 Downing Street, and the first to use the term 'Prime Minister' rather than 'First Lord of the Treasury'), he was succeeded by Herbert Henry Asquith (1852–1928), with whom Churchill was on good personal terms. David Lloyd George (1863–1945) was appointed to Asquith's old post as Chancellor and Churchill promoted to Lloyd George's perch at the Board of Trade. At thirty-three, he had arrived in the Cabinet at a younger age than even his father.

Affairs of the heart also intervened in Churchill's life during 1908. He had first met Clementine Hozier in 1904 at a ball. In March 1908, they met again when seated next to one another at a dinner party. After five months of meeting each other at social events, as well as a flurry of ardent letters, Winston proposed to Clemmie during a house party at Blenheim that summer, and they married on 12 September 1908 in the MPs' church of St Margaret's, Westminster, in the shadow of the Abbey, honeymooning in Venice and Moravia. Shortly afterwards, they set up home at 33 Eccleston Square, a four-storey Georgian townhouse in Pimlico, and it was here Diana and Randolph were born. Part of Churchill's genius was in picking strong characters to help him through various stages of his life. He was incredibly self-centred, with most who encountered him unable to penetrate the armour-plated layers of conceit with which he surrounded himself, for he often needed bringing back down to earth. Sonia Purnell reminds us Clemmie was the permanent fixture, to whom he listened and whom he obeyed for the rest of his life. More than anyone, it was she who crafted Churchill the politician, Prime Minister and warlord.

There was a rare energy in Asquith's 1908 Cabinet due to the burning ambitions of its two leading personalities, Churchill and Lloyd George. As unlike Churchill in background as it was possible to be, David Lloyd George was born into poor circumstances in Manchester but brought up in the Caernarfonshire village of Llanystumdwy, speaking Welsh as his first language. A fanatical Nonconformist and trained lawyer, he possessed – not unlike Churchill – quick wit and was capable of razor-sharp oratory, and set out to mentor Winston, who was nine years his junior. They became firm friends and a formidable double act, described as the 'terrible twins' by one contemporary. Historian Simon Schama has called them 'the hammer and the stiletto', with Churchill supplying the noise and Lloyd George the deadly knife. Thus, when Winston was Britain's premier in 1940–45, he knew exactly how to run a government and a country at war, having attentively watched his closest parliamentary colleague perform the same role in 1916–22.

The pair immediately shared concerns over the rise of Germany as a rival power, but admired Bismarck's bookkeeping, which had allowed Berlin to pay for both an impressive war fleet and pensions for the population. Churchill first gained his spurs as a social reformer with his May 1909 Labour Exchange Act, while Lloyd George unleashed his 'People's Budget' on 29 April, which placed an additional surcharge on higher incomes and dramatically hiked up death duties. Though passed by the House of Commons, the Lords rejected it on 30 November, clarifying they would pass the Budget only if the Liberals obtained an electoral mandate for so radical a series of innovations. The result was a constitutional crisis and the inconclusive general elections of January and December 1910. In both the nation faltered in its choice, but the Liberals remained, relying on Labour and Irish support. The star orator promoting his party and its policies around the country was Churchill, then seen by Conservatives as championing progressive causes and a traitor to his class, but it elevated him to national recognition.

From 3 to 11 December 1909 Churchill had been on the campaign trail, and in 1910 a distillation of his nine days of speeches, *The People's Rights* – which criticised the House of Lords and championed free trade, a graduated income tax, death duties and surtaxes on unearned income – was published in paperback. Churchill's oratorical efforts were not wasted, and he materially helped the Liberals to achieve a slim majority and passage of their Budget, which also led to the Parliament Act of 1911, depriving the House of Lords of its absolute power of veto on legislation. Churchill's reward from this lengthy political sparring, which he relished, was elevation to oversight of the Home Office aged thirty-five on 19 February 1910, making him the youngest occupier of this position since Peel in 1822. As Andrew Roberts notes, to date he remains 'the only home secretary... to have been sent to prison, let alone escaped from one'.

Though he would not be in office long, Churchill oversaw several important domestic skirmishes, chiefly against organised labour, which was becoming militant and had been infiltrated by extremists and their ideas, as elsewhere in Europe. Churchill's prominence also made him a particular target for the Women's Social and Political Union (WSPU), who disrupted his election meetings. Whatever sympathies he may have felt for the women's suffrage movement (due in part to his wife's support for their aims) evaporated on 15 November 1909, when one of their number set about him with a dog whip in Bristol's railway station. The *Manchester Guardian* reported:

> The full force of the blow fell upon his hat, but the lash cut Mr Churchill on the face. He turned immediately, and without hesitation seized the woman... She struggled, and as they were standing near the edge of the platform and in front of the space between two carriages it was a very exciting moment. The woman was shouting frantically, and was evidently beside herself... The words, 'Take that, you brute, you brute,' could be heard. Before the woman could make a further effort, Mr Churchill had wrenched the whip from her grasp. Then the police came and pinned her arms to her side.

A later Home Secretary and Churchill biographer, Roy Jenkins, wrote of discovering how hard Churchill worked in office, and how he was tortured in soul by the death sentences for capital crimes his office was then obliged to confirm. Despite presiding over much social reform, during the 1910–11 Cambrian Coal Strike Winston was forced to send London policemen and later troops to South Wales: first in November 1910, to assist the chief constable of Glamorgan protect private mine owners and their collieries from rioters at Tonypandy, and then in August 1911 to help keep order over striking railwaymen in Llanelli. In both places serious rioting caused deaths (though none at Tonypandy caused by soldiers firing on strikers, as is often alleged), which earned Churchill the unjust status of bloodthirsty tyrant among the radical left, a misplaced reputation which persists to this day.

Churchill also had to contend with the siege of Sidney Street of January 1911, a minor gunfight in London's East End between police and army personnel and two Latvian anarchists (as surmised from literature found after their deaths), the remnants of a gang who had murdered three policemen, wounding others while robbing a jewellery shop to fund Lenin and his Bolshevik movement. A small stand-off by contemporary standards, which lasted only six hours, but it was the first time London's Metropolitan Police had requested army help in the capital, and is best remembered for the flickering film of the Home Secretary, resplendent in Astrakhan coat and shining top hat, mingling with troops at the scene, made by an enterprising cameraman.

Instinctively drawn to the scent of shot and shell, Churchill's presence caused a political row and he later admitted his appearance was operationally inappropriate. The Tory opposition leader, Arthur Balfour, mused, 'I understand what the photographer was doing, but what was the Right Honourable Gentleman doing?' As Home Secretary, Winston had earlier been presented with a New Year's gift of a Webley pistol, but received it only after the Sidney Street incident. In his letter of thanks to the donor, he observed:

'Had it arrived just one day earlier it might have gone into action.' The drama was nevertheless a foretaste of Winston's inclination to eschew delegation, as well as an early indication of his desire for sartorial elegance in the most incongruous of circumstances.

A Cabinet reshuffle brought Churchill, seen as a good administrator and fearless reformer, appointment as First Lord of the Admiralty, the political head of the Royal Navy, on 25 October 1911 – 'The biggest thing that has ever come my way – the chance I should have chosen before all others,' thought its new incumbent. In those days, the position included use of the Admiralty luxury steam yacht *Enchantress* and, after taking up office, he set out to visit each capital ship and every Royal Navy base in the British Isles. He spent eight of his first twelve months in office aboard her, not just because he adored navy life, but, as Roy Jenkins has pointed out, also because the impecunious Churchills, with little private money, had difficulty making ends meet, even with a small entertainment allowance and house in Admiralty Arch. As it was assumed they had independent means, MPs were unsalaried until 1911, when they were initially paid a modest £400 a year. The solution was for the First Lord to conduct most of his business aboard his maritime manor, a Blenheim-of-the-waves. In 1912, *Enchantress* hove to opposite the former Greek colony of Paestum in southern Italy (precisely the area of the future Salerno beachhead of 1943), where he enlisted admirals Beatty and Masterton-Smith to join him in a lizard hunt. He summed up his approach to life with his observation, 'As with all things, there is a science to catching lizards and we must now master it.'

The navy's professional head, the dynamic but aged Admiral Jackie Fisher (1841–1920), had just retired. As First Sea Lord between 1904 and 1910, Fisher had overseen most of the numerous reforms which transformed this valuable tool of empire from the status of a museum of oaken relics to the foremost fighting fleet in the world. His sixty years' service had witnessed the replacement of shot-and-sail men-of-war with sleek, steel-hulled battleships, bearing breech-loading guns in revolving turrets, most notably the revolutionary *Dreadnought*, launched in 1906. Her twelve-inch guns paired in five turrets could take on and destroy an opponent at over nine miles. On his watch, Churchill was determined to ensure Fisher's remaining ideas were implemented as the rest of the world's war fleets woke up to the possibilities of modern technologies and started snapping at Britain's heels. For, as the newly appointed Winston observed: 'The usefulness of a naval invention ceases when it is enjoyed by everyone else.' In the pre-war dreadnought race, the public cry was taken up: 'We want eight and we won't wait' (for new warships). The result was hardly a surprise, as Churchill wryly noted: 'The Admiralty demanded six ships; the economists offered four; and we finally compromised on eight.'

'Installed by Asquith to get a political grip on spendthrift sailors, Winston was soon captivated by the romance of the senior service,' notes Richard Holmes. He had Clemmie christen the first battleship of his tenure *Centurion*; another, the *Benbow*, by his mother, and named two more, *Marlborough* and *Ramillies*, in honour of his ducal ancestor. Having up-gunned elements of the fleet from 12- and 13.5- to 15-inch main weaponry, in December 1913 Churchill insisted on more money to expand the Royal Navy, but was opposed in Cabinet by his close friend, the mercurial Lloyd George. The bickering was brutal and left Churchill feeling betrayed, but eventually he prevailed. Winston then had to persuade the entire House of Commons of the wisdom of slowing further domestic reforms in favour of more weapons. The 'guns or butter' debate has never gone down well with peaceable Britons, and never less so than in early 1914, with few war clouds on the immediate horizon. Regarded by some Conservative, Liberal and Labour MPs as a warmonger, Churchill, in a mammoth three-hour speech on 17 March 1914, won enough round and got his money for increasing the naval estimates. The First Lord thus read the international tea leaves more correctly than any in the Cabinet – save the Foreign Secretary, Sir Edward Grey.

Both had worked out that any German aggression against France would likely advance through neutral Belgium and thus amount to a threat to the United Kingdom. While the assassination of the Austrian archduke in Sarajevo on 28 June 1914 initiated the sequence of events which led to the First World War, it was at dusk on 3 August, as Grey was looking out of his room in the Foreign Office, that he turned to a friend and remarked: 'The lamps are going out all over Europe; we shall not see them lit again in our lifetime.'

Churchill's prescience of impending catastrophe beat Grey by a week. On 15 July he had initiated a routine test mobilisation of the Home Fleet, but as it ended, and with the Balkan crisis unresolved, Churchill decided on his own authority not to disperse his vessels. More concerned than ever, on 27 July he sent out pre-war warnings, and two days later ordered ships to their war stations. At the same moment, Churchill wrote to his wife of his guilt: 'Everything tends towards catastrophe and collapse. I am interested, geared up and happy. Is it not horrible to be built like that? The preparations have a hideous fascination for me. I pray to God to forgive me for such fearful moods of levity.'

Principal among Fisher's aspirations was a switch from coal propulsion (which required a costly network of coaling stations around the world, and vast armies of men to shovel the black stuff about) to that of oil. In 1912 Churchill had appointed Fisher chairman of the Royal Commission on Fuel and Engines, and in 1914, with visionary zeal, Winston insisted Britain purchase 51 per cent of the Anglo-Persian Oil Company, effectively nationalising the corporation which had been founded in 1909. Its ramifications were a permanent British (and later American) interest in the Middle East, one still prevalent today, and a further demise of the domestic coal industry, and it ensured when Britain went to war on 4 August 1914, Churchill's fleet was the most modern in the world, and ready for action.

CHAPTER 3

World Crisis

C HURCHILL'S major contribution to policy during the
First World War is always assumed to be initiating the
Gallipoli campaign of 1915. The reality was he had more
military background than anyone else in Cabinet (excepting
Kitchener, brought in as Secretary of State for War on 5
August, but who had no experience of Cabinet government).
Thus it was the First Lord of the Admiralty who attempted
to run the war single-handedly, treading on the toes of every
department when the mood took him. In October 1914 he
visited Antwerp, still in Allied hands, took command of
its defences, then sent a bizarre note to Asquith offering to
resign from the Admiralty and stay at the front. This was
the former Lieutenant Churchill begging to be appointed
General Churchill, a position for which he had no training,
and, in reality, in search of another war to fight. Rightly, he
was given short shrift, although he did form a Royal Naval
Division from excess maritime personnel and marines, which
would fight with distinction on land as the 63rd Division.

Yet Churchill had a point about military experience and was able to dominate many Cabinet sessions when discussing military policy. He pushed for the development of naval aviation and carriers (he had taken flying lessons in 1912, until Clemmie learned his instructor had died in a flying accident), coined the word 'seaplane', and oversaw the official birth of the Royal Naval Air Service in 1914 – which merged with the Royal Flying Corps to form the Royal Air Force in 1918 – something which would lead to his appointment as Honorary Air Commodore of No. 615 (County of Surrey) Squadron, Royal Auxiliary Air Force in 1939. Although he never qualified as a pilot, he often wandered onto the flight deck of aircraft shuttling him about, and, on 1 April 1943, would be awarded honorary 'wings' in acknowledgement of all he had done for military aviation.

Meanwhile, Churchill's technical curiosity led him to dragoon the army into exploring the concept of 'land ironclads' (an idea borrowed from the writer H. G. Wells, whom he had invited to the Other Club), later to emerge as the world's first tanks, while he deluged other ministries with papers and studies far beyond his remit. Asquith's fault was to let him get away with it. There was no war cabinet, strategy being conducted by twenty-one ministries in 1914, and twenty-three in 1916, which would prove to be the Prime Minister's undoing.

In October 1914, Churchill recalled Fisher as First Sea Lord, the navy's professional head, after Prince Louis of Battenberg (married to a granddaughter of Queen Victoria and father of Lord Louis Mountbatten) retired due to his ancestry as a foreign prince, at a time when anti-German sentiment was running high. About to enter his seventy-fifth year, the crotchety but forthright Fisher proved to be an older version of Churchill, in his energy, zeal, foresight and innovative thinking. He was another, like Clemmie, who could penetrate the younger man's armour. Alike in temperament, they clashed often, but the pair worked out that, with deadlock soon achieved on the Western Front, a war-winning strategy needed to be found elsewhere.

'Are there not other alternatives than sending our armies to chew barbed wire in Flanders?' mused Winston. Both knew their maps and charts and soon alighted on the Turkish-controlled Dardanelles, the narrow strait separating the Mediterranean from the Black Sea, and Europe from Asia, as a promising area for military activity. Fleet action to seize the waterway from control of Turkey, an Austro-German partner, could lead to the capture of its capital, Constantinople (now Istanbul), secure a supply route to their Anglo-French ally Russia, help reinforce the Eastern Front and persuade Romania to join the Allied cause.

It was a valid, but disastrously executed, strategy, one which came at the wrong time. Here the ghost of Churchill's poor relations with Kitchener came into play, for the general refused to release army manpower, and an impatient Churchill threw an Anglo-French fleet alone at the Turkish defences on 19 February 1915. They might have succeeded if accompanied by a land force, but under their opponents' Krupp-supplied heavy artillery, Allied minesweepers failed in their task, and on 18 March the fleet lost three large battleships to mines, *Irresistible*, *Ocean* and the French *Bouvet*, with three others seriously damaged, and refused to press home their attack. A pause then ensued while several army formations (including his own Royal Naval Division) assembled, which, with French infantry and the Australian and New Zealand Army Corps (ANZAC), made amphibious landings on 25 April. However, where there had been few Turkish defenders in February, the same terrain bristled with hostile weaponry and men by the time the boys from Britain, France and the Antipodes arrived. Irrespective of the muddle and disaster Gallipoli became, the presence of the army signified Churchill was no longer in control.

Fisher resigned on 15 May 1915 amid bitter arguments over Gallipoli, having earlier scribbled a note to his master exclaiming 'Damn the Dardanelles' and correctly forecasting the operation would 'be their grave'. Despite further landings, and hampered by the lack of any amphibious warfare doctrine, which meant local commanders were making poor operational decisions on the hoof, the campaign soon drifted into helpless stalemate and chewed up precisely the scarce manpower and resources it was meant to save from absorption into the Western Front. Finding his brother Jack was at Gallipoli, Winston had written to him on 19 April: 'The vital thing is not to break off because of losses but to persevere. This is the hour in the world's history for a fine feat of arms, and the results of victory will amply justify the price.'

Despite Churchill's continued optimism, the force was withdrawn in January 1916, one of the last officers to leave being Major Clement Attlee, but it had suffered huge casualties. Gallipoli forced a crisis of confidence in London, causing Asquith, in May 1915, to enter a coalition with his Conservative opponents, who demanded Churchill, as the expedition's author, resign. A compromise was reached, in which Churchill was demoted from First Lord, thus losing his beloved home in Admiralty Arch, and the most significant pre-Prime Ministerial job of his political life, but he remained in Cabinet as Chancellor of the Duchy of Lancaster. The Churchills thereupon decamped to Hoe Farm, a sixteenth-century mansion near Godalming, Surrey, rented jointly with his brother Jack, on which the architect Sir Edwin Lutyens had once dabbled. With its serene views, four reception rooms and eight bedrooms, gardens, paddocks, stables and tennis court, it would become the inspiration for Winston's own Chartwell.

His time at the Admiralty had brought Churchill a wider insight into the mechanics of fighting and winning a global war than any other portfolio could have done. Despite its defeat, he took away much from the Gallipoli landings and campaign, including the need for air–maritime–land co-operation, amphibious doctrine with specialised landing craft, and exhaustive reconnaissance and intelligence preparation; the importance of choosing appropriate commanders; and the necessity of surprise and of a generous lead time for thorough pre-invasion training and rehearsals. Gallipoli would induce in him an understandable sense of foreboding about the Normandy landings of June 1944, but, once forced to commit himself by the Americans, Churchill was at least sustained by knowing what *not* to do as a result of the Dardanelles. Although the big fleet encounter at Jutland (31 May–1 June 1916), the emergence of the German U-boat menace in 1917 – necessitating home-front rationing – and its countering with convoys and depth charges were after his time at the Admiralty, he stayed in touch with naval developments. All would be repeated in the Second World War, with the difference that Churchill, initially as First Lord again in 1939, alone of all politicians (save the dying Lloyd George) would know what to do and how to do it.

He hung on for much of the year, though feeling 'like a sea-beast fished up from the depths, or a diver too suddenly hoisted', and was prompted at Hoe Farm by his brother Jack's wife Gwendoline (Goonie) to take up painting with oils to combat the stress of inactivity. Modern decision-makers may choose to work out in a gymnasium, but Churchill's stress-busting equivalent was to daub oil on canvas, at which he became quite proficient. Other artists have called his work naive, but his works, rendered in an impressionist style, are pleasing to the eye, such as the picture of Marrakech. However, this is putting a positive gloss on Winston's post-Gallipoli mood, for Clemmie observed much later: 'The Dardanelles haunted him for the rest of his life. He always believed in it. When he left the Admiralty, he thought he was finished. I thought he would never get over the Dardanelles; I thought he would die of grief.'

It was an instance of the depression which sometimes crossed his path when successes were followed by plunging lows. Churchill nicknamed it his 'black dog'. Arguably, Winston's absurdly busy, action-packed life, accompanied by endless entertaining, writing, speechifying and politicking, and punctuated by a bizarre array of hobbies and pastimes, was the Churchillian way of keeping at bay a longer-term, deeper depressive condition. He was born into an era when adults rarely discussed their inner turmoil, and would have been ever watchful of his own psychological state, having witnessed Lord Randolph's mental decline.

Though biographer Andrew Roberts cautions against making too much of the 'black dog', and Winston clearly enjoyed his many activities, they may also represent his coping mechanism against failure. This moment also initiated his 'keep buggering on' attitude to life when faced with setbacks of any description. Often abbreviated in private correspondence and speech to 'KBO', female friends and staff were rewarded with a sanitised version: 'Keep plodding on,' or 'KPO'.

'Always endeavour to turn catastrophe to your own advantage,' he wrote, and, on 12 November 1915, Churchill did just this in penning a note to Asquith resigning from the government, but not from Parliament. He signed off: 'Count on me absolutely – if I am of any use. If not, some employment in the field.' In fact, Winston had already made plans to serve on the Western Front, hoping to command a brigade or a division, but accepted he needed first to 'bed in', leading first a company (of the 2nd Grenadier Guards), then a Kitchener battalion (the 6th Royal Scots Fusiliers) early in 1916.

His official biographer, Martin Gilbert, records Winston's round of final dinner parties before leaving for Flanders as resembling a wake, as though he intended to commit suicide by launching himself into battle. In the event, he proved an excellent infantry commander, joining his Royal Scots Fusiliers at Ploegsteert in Belgium. His mood changed instantly, as he revelled in front-line life, instructing his officers: 'War is a game that is played with a smile. If you can't smile, grin. If you can't grin, keep out of the way till you can.' Going to war can be a liberating experience as the individual frees themselves of personal and professional woes and ties up their affairs in the event of death. Churchill certainly felt this, and, accompanied by his paintbox and the sound of German guns, wrote to his mother: 'I am happy here... I always get on with soldiers. I do not certainly regret the step I took... I know that I am doing the right thing... Do you know I am quite young again?'

Sustained by supplies from Fortnum & Mason, Churchill enjoyed a 'good war', sharing the hardships of trench life (and his hampers) with his Glaswegian troops, who had answered the patriotic call to arms of August 1914. His command was no sinecure, for Winston's battalion had suffered greatly the previous September at the Battle of Loos, and needed a repair of morale and rebuilding to full strength, while his 9th (Scottish) Division was the first of Kitchener's all-volunteer army to serve on the Western Front. The Military Service Act of 27 January 1916, the inaugural introduction of conscription to the United Kingdom, would see its draftees arrive only after Churchill had left soldiering and returned to politics.

Introducing himself with the words, 'Gentlemen, I am now your Commanding Officer. Those who support me I will look after. Those who go against me I will break,' Winston drove his battalion hard in training, resulting in their losses being lower than the rest of the Scottish Division. He proved a predictably fearless leader, personally patrolling the front lines and surviving several close calls. However, after 108 days in command, when his battalion was amalgamated with its sister 7th Battalion and, on 7 May 1916, transferred to a different brigade, of the 15th (Scottish) Division, Churchill made no attempt to request a new command, still feeling the lure of politics and pull of Westminster in his bones. Of the farewell from his battalion, adjutant Andrew Dewar Gibb (author of *With Winston Churchill at the Front*, written in 1924 under the pseudonym 'Captain X'), recorded: 'I believe every man in the room felt Winston Churchill's leaving us a real personal loss.'

Winston had long realised his preference for being at the helm, shaping events, over being a passenger in them. Kitchener (to be drowned at sea on 5 June 1916), Field Marshal Douglas Haig and the rest of Britain's military hierarchy breathed a sigh of relief at his departure. Ever the individualist, who sported a French military helmet in preference to the British-issued 'battle bowler', Churchill made friends everywhere, but his superiors regarded his passion and curiosity for wartime innovation, and his bypassing of the chain of command when it suited him, as being at least as dangerous as the German army lurking across no man's land. Winston was again lucky, for had he remained with the 15th (Scottish) Division, he would have been sucked into the struggle for the Somme, beginning on 1 July. His division lost 1,901 men in four separate battles, of whom 137 were from his old battalion.

Asquith, meanwhile, was perceived to be steering a rudderless ship in wartime, and to be distracted by the death of his eldest son, Raymond, killed on 15 September 1916 at Flers–Courcelette, on the Somme. Partly blamed for Gallipoli and other disasters, he was replaced on 6 December in a Westminster coup. Lloyd George had been agitating for a small war cabinet (then called a war council) under his own authority, with the Conservatives in the coalition threatening to resign unless his plan was implemented. After many behind-the-scenes political machinations, Lloyd George negotiated a five-man war cabinet, formed a new administration and kissed hands with the King, becoming Prime Minister on the morning of 7 December.

Although the Conservatives explicitly demanded Churchill be excluded from ministerial office, Lloyd George was aware of his friend's organising talents and opportunistic zeal, and, seven months later, felt secure enough to appoint Winston to the Cabinet-level (but not war cabinet) post of Minister of Munitions on 17 July 1917. He was joined there by Asquith's third son, Arthur, who had served in the Royal Naval Division on Gallipoli and elsewhere, won three DSOs and attained the rank of brigadier general, but lost a leg and was invalided out of the service. The ministry was a wartime stopgap, established on 25 May 1915 to overcome the 'Shell Crisis' of the same year, which occurred in response to newspaper criticism of severe military shortages, and affected all the belligerents at this time. Initially under Lloyd George's vigorous leadership, and crucial to his rise to supreme power, the ministry soon set up a nationwide network of factories; staffed them with women (encouraged into war work by higher rates of pay than received by their absent menfolk); created a system to resolve labour disputes; breathed new life into cumbersome War Office bureaucracy; promoted factory safety (though disasters from mishandling explosives occurred); provided day care for children; limited overtime; provided transportation and lodging for some workers; and crucially oversaw a dramatic expansion in the production of weaponry and ammunition.

The ministry was less than two years old, and Churchill would be its fourth minister, but the post was no sinecure, for by the war's end it possessed a central staff of 65,000, employed 3 million workers in over 20,000 factories, including 218 purpose-built, and had become the nation's largest buyer, seller and employer. As he observed at the time: 'This is a very heavy department, almost as interesting as the Admiralty, with the enormous advantage one has neither got to fight Admirals nor Huns!' The ministry's template for industrial change management, reform and rationalisation remains one to which experts still return, over 100 years later. Despite fervent Conservative hostility to his appointment, Churchill delivered, and the portfolio brought him formally what he had been trying to achieve informally at the Admiralty: coordination with every ministry involved in the pursuit of war and cooperation with Allied nations. It also set a host of precedents which would prove vital to him in 1940, such as the centralisation of war-manufacturing and wholesale induction of women into previously men-only trades. By the war's end, in its brief life the ministry had overseen the production of 3,000 tanks, 75 million Mills bombs, 4 million rifles, a quarter of a million machine guns, 52,000 aeroplanes, 25,000 artillery pieces and over 170 million artillery shells.

At this time Winston met Siegfried Sassoon, then a recent recipient of a Military Cross won on the Somme. The war poet recalled Churchill 'gave me an emphatic vindication of militarism as an instrument of policy and stimulator of glorious individual achievements'. At the conclusion, Sassoon was left musing on whether Churchill had been entirely serious when he observed: 'War is the normal occupation of man.' 'It had been unmistakable that for him war was the finest activity on earth.' This assertion does not put Churchill in the category of warmonger, but one senses the relish with which Winston attacked any task which embraced military activity. It also implied a deeper understanding of the nature of war than was possessed by any of his contemporaries.

Winston naturally made use of every opportunity to explore the front, Douglas Haig arranging for the Château de Verchocq, near his own headquarters at Montreuil, to be placed at Churchill's disposal. He was staying with his old 9th Division when the last German offensive of 21 March 1918 began. 'The flame of the bombardment lit like flickering firelight in my tiny cabin,' he wrote, escaping in the nick of time. He conveyed the seriousness of the situation to London, helping to trigger reinforcements flowing into France. On 10 August he wrote to Clemmie of his satisfaction over the victory at Amiens, just fought. This was, then and now, generally regarded as the turning point of the war, when the British Army came of age. Churchill by then would have understood that operational success involved the coordination of aircraft, artillery, armour and infantry, and was pleased to have, through his Admiralty and Munitions portfolios, which gave him opportunities to further the development of armoured vehicles, aircraft and other pet devices of war, played his part in it. As he mused: 'It is our victory, won... largely through the invincible tank.'

Yet the war still had three months to run. On 28 October, Churchill, as Minister of Munitions, with brother Jack attended a victory parade in the newly liberated French city of Lille. A photographer captured them reviewing the march-past of the 47th (London) Division in the Grand Place. In the foreground is the division's chief of staff, to whom he had just been introduced, one Lieutenant Colonel Bernard Montgomery, each obviously unaware of the crucial role he would play in the other's life.

When the end came, on 11 November, it was brutally abrupt. The overall feeling was, as Charles Carrington, a literary-minded officer of the Royal Warwicks, observed: 'In 1918 we had not been sure even of eventual victory till the late summer, and had seen no hope of a quick ending to the war until three or four weeks before it happened. Victory was sudden and complete and the general sensation was of awaking from a nightmare.' Winston dined at No. 10 with Lloyd George, who proposed to execute the Kaiser. Churchill demurred and, aware that the menace of Bolshevism was threatening to subsume Germany, suggested loading a dozen great ships with provisions and expediting them to Hamburg. Perhaps his more humane approach might have removed one cause of the Nazis' later rise to power.

CHAPTER 4

Roving Commissions

O N 10 January 1919 Lloyd George shifted Churchill to become Secretary of State for War, a position he himself had held from Kitchener's unexpected death in June 1916 until becoming Prime Minister. The portfolio later included air; thus, uniquely, Winston presided over each of the three services. This was probably the key ministry of the hour, grappling with downsizing budgets and personnel, payment of end-of-service gratuities, and fears of, in Carrington's words, the 'spread of Bolshevism in the ranks, more prevalent among "base wallahs" than front line troops'. Whitehall had already been invaded by mobs of servicemen who had seized army lorries and driven to London to demonstrate outside the War Office at their slow release. Ignoring Haig's rational plan for demobilisation, bureaucrats had commenced discharging soldiers according to industrial and economic needs, which produced some very odd results. In one case, a farm labourer, who had entered 'farm assist' as his profession on his call-up paperwork, found himself speedily discharged with a group of pharmacists.

Sensing rising disorder, Churchill quickly switched to Haig's trusted metrics of release by wounds, age, length of service, marriage status and bravery awards. Many warriors who had proved themselves, such as this writer's maternal grandfather, were given access to and support for study at universities, a turn of events not remotely imaginable to them four years earlier; others were offered land and money to settle in the colonies. The very youngest, having progressed straight from school into khaki, and suddenly released from the gut-twisting tension of front-line duties, acquired a perfectly justifiable fear of unemployment, knowing no other way to earn a wage.

The new minister quickly raised rates of pay for serving soldiers and offered bounties to those who would re-enlist, in order to recruit an army of occupation along the German Rhineland. Facsimiles of Churchill's signature appeared on all the post-Armistice awards for gallantry, mentions in dispatches and acknowledgements of service, thus tying his name closely to the personal military histories of an entire generation of servicemen. Of his new political boss, Haig felt moved to record in his private journal on 15 January 1919:

> I thought Churchill showed up well at this conference [held in London to discuss a future army of occupation in Germany] and by taking this great responsibility so soon... he made it clear... he not only has courage, but foresight and a knowledge of statesmanship. All of these

qualities most of his colleagues seem to have lacked so
lamentably throughout this war.

If asked, many of the 8.7 million who passed through the
ranks of the army at some stage during 1914–18, not a few
plucked from industrial slums, would have owned up to
benefiting from the regular meals, frequent medical checks,
occasional dentistry, camaraderie, and decent clothing and
boots their army had given them. Where assessed, the average
male of 1919–20 was an inch or two taller, a stone heavier
and in overall better health than his predecessor of six years
earlier.

While such benefits may have been pathetic recompense
for being shelled and shot at, or for the million posted dead
or missing, for the surviving participants the Great War was
not nearly as disenchanting as later historians would have
us believe. When Field Marshal Haig died of a heart attack
in January 1928, the media of the day reported a million
of his former soldiers lined the route for his state funeral in
Westminster Abbey. There was a limited wave of war disil-
lusionment which crept into public consciousness ten years
on from the Armistice, led by German veteran Erich Maria
Remarque's 1928 novel *Im Westen nichts Neues* which sold
a million copies, and another million when translated into
English as *All Quiet on the Western Front*. The first of its
three film adaptions appeared in 1930. Richard Aldington,
Edmund Blunden, Vera Brittain, Ernest Hemingway, Siegfried
Sassoon, Ernst Jünger and R. C. Sherriff's memorable play
Journey's End added to the barrage of memoirs and anti-
war fiction during the 1928–33 period, but further analysis

was deflected by the new Nazi threat and, in 1939, by the outbreak of another world war, and only resumed in the 1960s, by which time history was dominated by a rebellious anti-war school.[*]

All the while, Churchill's ministry was battling with another enemy, one which would prove more deadly than the war just finished. In March 1918 a case of killer influenza had been reported in Kansas, and as huge numbers of American servicemen flowed across the Atlantic, more cases were soon detected in France and the United Kingdom. Wartime censors suppressed the news to maintain morale, but neutral Spanish newspapers freely reported the outbreak, hence the contagion becoming known as 'Spanish flu'. Two years later, nearly a third of the global population, or an estimated 500 million people, had been infected in four successive waves, killing between 20 and 40 million, certainly more than the 17 million felled in the late war. Unlike normal influenza epidemics, which only affect the old and very young, this strain attacked hitherto healthy young adults, including soldiers.

It affected the Churchill family, then living at 2 Sussex Square, London W2, with Clemmie and three of her children falling ill; they survived, but Isabelle, the children's Scottish

---

[*] In their midst, on 20 October 1930 Winston's autobiography, *My Early Life*, arrived. Though partly a war memoir, it described a much earlier era, aware that the recent conflict had destroyed the world into which he had been born. Written with nostalgia and sentimentality, it made no reference to 1914–18, and was thus almost a two-fingered salute to the many grim accounts on the bookshelves. Instead, *My Early Life* offered a romantic view of Churchill's past. Its last sentence concluded that in September 1908 he 'married and lived happily ever after'. Thus, Winston self-consciously penned a fairy story, albeit true, about himself – for which reason it sold well then, and has done ever since.

nanny, passed away. Winston, meanwhile, was in Cannes, beginning work on his history of recent events, entitled *The World Crisis*. Many wives would have objected to their partner's absence, but the ever-stoical Clemmie wrote: 'It is providential you went away as it would have been most annoying if you had caught it. I do hope you are having a delicious time.' Winston responded: 'What a cataclysm! Poor darling. I expect you have had an awful time. But as usual you have risen to the occasion and your letter about it all is Napoleonic.'

After the signing of the Treaty of Versailles, a day of festivity, Victory Day, was announced for 19 July 1919. London was decorated as for a coronation and Churchill arranged a nine-mile parade of troops, all bearing their regimental colours, and representatives of every cap badge in the British and empire forces, with contingents of foreign allies and tanks adding further colour to the procession. It may seem counter-intuitive today, but the loudest cheers were reportedly reserved for the Frenchman Ferdinand Foch, Allied generalissimo, and Haig, Britain's commander-in-chief. Uniquely, Churchill had both directed part of the wartime drama and – through his leadership of the 6th Royal Scots Fusiliers – been in it, something which would bring him great credibility with the warriors of Britain.

He also conferred about the future of the legions of old comrades' associations and ex-servicemen's groups springing up around the country. Trade unions wished to recruit some, while others foresaw a political role for themselves, rather like the ultra-right *Stahlhelm* ('Steel Helmet') in troubled Germany, which would breed the Nazi Party. Eventually, the National Federation of Discharged Soldiers and Sailors and the Comrades of the Great War, which reflected the left and right of politics, respectively, and the centrist National Union of Ex-Servicemen, were directed into the non-political British Legion, a happy ending for which Haig and Churchill could take credit.

As Lloyd George's fireman, but also now his younger rival, Churchill found himself at the Colonial Office on 13 February 1921, a promotion from the first government position he had held between 1905 and 1908 in the same ministry. It physically removed him from Lloyd George (whose reputation was fast being tarnished by his chasing of women and selling of honours) and London, as the former intended, and forced Winston to focus on Middle Eastern oil, the Suez Canal and post-Ottoman Arab kingdoms, allowing him renewed acquaintanceship with Egypt and the Sudan. It brought him into contact with the Arabist Colonel T. E. Lawrence and archaeologist Gertrude Bell. Simon Schama ventures the view that this brought out 'the "true" Churchill, the aristocratic reactionary, reverting to type after his brief, uncharacteristic fling with social reform'.

The reverse might equally be true, argues Andrew Roberts: Churchill was a political doppelgänger of his father, at heart a Tory democrat, a progressive social liberal and reformer, though his inner historian was almost blindly attracted to monarchies and monarchs. Hence, his oft-stated wish to strangle Bolshevism, with its communist offshoot, at birth. Paradoxically, Winston was also an imperialist, hostile for most of his career to progressive colonial independence, especially for India, which he saw as Britain's prop to economic survival, military power and international prestige. None were particularly retrograde tendencies, as some modern historians argue, but rational, if old-fashioned, reactions to the challenges of his era, with its notions of the validity of Great Powers, fragile crowns and swaggering aristocrats.

The fate of Palestine dogged much of his tenure at the Colonial Office in 1921–22, which saw played out Britain's long-term commitment to the terms of the Balfour Declaration of 2 November 1917. Winston was unique in his collection of Jewish friends, at a time when Britain's ruling classes were riddled with anti-Semitic sentiment. Although it didn't necessarily advance British interests, Churchill more than any other government figure implemented the declaration, which ensured Jews possessed the right to emigrate to Palestine, and insisted to Palestinian Arabs they accept it. It would set in motion the founding of the state of Israel in 1948. He saw a pro-British Palestine as an insurance policy for the Suez Canal, itself garrisoned with imperial troops, telling the Commons in July 1922, 'Palestine is all the more important to us... in view of the ever-growing significance of the Suez Canal; and I do not think £1,000,000 a year... would be too much for Great Britain to pay for the control and guardianship of this great historic land.'

Despite the lobbying of T. E. Lawrence and his fellow Arabists, which brought about the detachment of Transjordan as a separate kingdom and the creation of Iraq out of Mesopotamia at the Cairo Conference of March 1921 (how different this was from the subsequent Cairo gathering in 1943, attended by Chiang Kai-shek and Roosevelt, which underlined the tilt of power away from Britain), Churchill also believed, betraying a soupçon of ignorant prejudice, European Jews would 'civilise the Muslims of the Levant'. To the Commons he argued Zionist efforts to develop Palestine brought 'life to the desert wastes and new money into the country, with assurance of a greater prosperity and means of a higher economic and social life'.

Yet Winston also worried that some European Jews, flirting with revolutionary politics and anarchy, might carry 'political infection into Palestine under the guise of Zionism', hence he often blew hot and cold over the advantages of the Balfour Declaration. Along the way, he had to overcome challenges of reducing expenditure while keeping order in Turkey, Mesopotamia and Persia. 'Do please realise everything else that happens in the Middle East is secondary to the reduction of expense,' Churchill felt obliged to minute in mid-1920, while bemoaning his belief that 'things were not going to get better in this part of the world, but rather worse'. Onlookers were amazed to discover, by the time of his departure from office, he had managed to reduce Middle East expenditure by a creditable 75 per cent from its 1920 level, often via imposing control by armed aircraft instead of by land forces. Churchill's perceived even-handedness in Palestine was rewarded in 1940–42, when local troops of the British Palestine Regiment were deployed to defend Suez and combat the Vichy French in Syria, while a larger Jewish brigade would fight in Italy during 1944–45.

In 1922 the coalition which had been fraying since the war's end finally broke apart, leading to a general election on 15 November. This produced the odd result of political re-alignment, with Lloyd George's credibility exhausted and the Liberal vote plummeting, taking them to third-party status, and power henceforth being shared between the Conservative and Labour parties. Churchill, who had moved constituencies from Oldham to another urban centre, Dundee, in 1908 after his defection to the Liberals, was but one casualty of many, losing by 10,000 votes. He was ill with appendicitis at the time, forcing Clemmie to campaign on his behalf.

After the election result, he was able to reflect: 'In the twinkling of an eye, I found myself without an office, without a seat, without a party and without an appendix.' Undeterred, for Gallipoli had taught him a valuable lesson in coping with adversity (which, as in 1945, the formidable Clemmie called 'a blessing in disguise', to which her husband responded: 'It is certainly very well disguised'), he contested constituencies in Leicester West (1923) and Westminster Abbey (1924), before finding a new political home in the north London seat of Epping at the 1924 general election, winning with a comfortable 10,000 majority – the amount by which he had lost at Dundee. In each case, however, Churchill campaigned as a 'Constitutionalist', his name still anathema to the Tory cause. In 1945, Epping's boundaries were redrawn to form most of the new Woodford constituency, which he would represent for the rest of his political life, and as a Conservative.

Meanwhile, he had negotiated a £42,000 advance to write *The World Crisis*, his war memoirs, which eventually ran to six volumes (1923–31), and rent Villa Rêve d'Or, near Cannes, to where he and Clemmie (when recovered from her Spanish flu) temporarily retired. This allowed him to write and paint, while dashing back to fight the occasional election. Thus began the Churchills' long love affair with the Côte d'Azur and one of the most relaxed periods of his life:

his many ultramarine canvases of the Mediterranean, various villas, and cypress and olive trees reflect this inner calm. 'The painter wanders and loiters contentedly from place to place, always on the lookout for some brilliant butterfly of a picture which can be caught and set up and carried safely home,' he observed of his growing skills on canvas. 'Time stands respectfully aside, and it is only after many hesitations that luncheon knocks gruffly at the door.' Southern France was also important for another reason: the year 1921 had proven to be the Churchills' annus horribilis. In April, Clemmie's brother Bill committed suicide; Winston's beloved mother, Jennie, died aged sixty-seven in June, and, on 23 August, their daughter Marigold succumbed to septicaemia. However, as Winston had already exceeded Lord Randolph's forty-five-year lifespan, he had slain the private fear that he would die as young as his father.

Meanwhile, Churchill the superior scribe would use *The World Crisis* to justify the Dardanelles campaign. It was well received, though one political wag (Arthur Balfour) described it as 'an autobiography disguised as a history of the universe', stating: 'Winston had written an enormous book about himself, and called it *The World Crisis*.' With his rhetorical flourishes and cutting analysis, it is in many ways better than his *Second World War* history, which, adopting a more reportage-like approach, was written by teams of experts and polished by Churchill, as we shall see. In *The World Crisis*, Winston the wordsmith is more evident, even if there is a varnish of self-justification over Gallipoli. Historian Robert Rhodes James opined: 'For all its pitfalls as history, [it] must surely stand as Churchill's masterpiece.'

The October 1924 general election, with its Conservative landslide, interrupted the Churchills' peace. Although elected for Epping as a Constitutionalist, he and the new Tory leader, Stanley Baldwin (1867–1947), had put out peace feelers, and Winston was formally readmitted into the Conservative Party, symbolically recrossing the floor of the Commons and observing sardonically of his own behaviour: 'Anyone can rat, but it takes a certain ingenuity to re-rat.' Baldwin rewarded him with his father's old post, held thirty-eight years before, of Chancellor of the Exchequer, to the great surprise of many. This would amount to Winston's first period of residence in Downing Street (where Chancellors traditionally reside, at No. 11), but he was dumbfounded at the offer, recording:

> I was shown into the Prime Minister's office. After a few commonplaces I asked him whether he minded the smoke of a cigar. He said 'No,' and pulled out his famous pipe. Then he said, 'Are you willing to help us?' I replied guardedly, 'Yes, if you really want me.' I had no intention of joining the Government except in some great position, and I had no idea – nor had anyone else – what was in his mind. So when he said, 'Will you be Chancellor of the Exchequer?' I was astonished. I had never dreamed my credit with him stood so high... I should have liked to have answered, 'Will the bloody duck swim?' but as it was a formal and important conversation I replied, 'This fulfils my ambition. I still have my father's robe as Chancellor. I shall be proud to serve you in this splendid Office.'

After accepting the post, his first major decision was the restoration of the gold standard at its pre-First World War parity of $4.86 to the pound, which he announced in his first Budget statement of April 1925. This decision was greeted with approval by the Bank of England and party colleagues, but economists such as John Maynard Keynes (in the 1925 pamphlet *The Economic Consequences of Mr Churchill*) warned, correctly as it turned out, such a measure would seriously damage Britain's major export industries of coal mining, shipbuilding, and textile and steel manufacture, and result in deflation and unemployment. Mine owners soon demanded longer hours for less pay, forcing Churchill to introduce a subsidy for the industry to prevent the reduction of wages as a result of lower turnover. This led to a coal strike, for which he became the intermediary between striking miners and mine owners, proposing any lowering of wages be paralleled by a reduction in the owners' profits. However, no compromise could be reached, and a ten-day General Strike followed later, called by the Trades Union Congress. Throughout 3–12 May 1926, Churchill marshalled his resources to oppose it, as though back at the Admiralty, commandeering printing presses and editing a government propaganda news sheet, the *British Gazette*, in opposition to the TUC's *British Worker*.

He wrote many of its articles while troops delivered food supplies and undergraduates staffed public transport. Baldwin made a national broadcast on the new BBC, founded in 1922, coached by its puritanical managing director (later director general), John Reith, an acerbic Scotsman who wore a prominent scar on his left cheek from his service on the Western

Front. When the Labour leader, Ramsay MacDonald (1866–1937), wanted to respond, Reith supported the request, but was refused by Baldwin. Thereafter Reith determined to keep his organisation independent, deciding self-censorship was the best way forward, and refused airtime even to a conciliatory statement by the Archbishop of Canterbury.

Reith was canny enough to use the newspaper silence to launch his own roving reporting operations, the origin of today's outside news teams. Although it was the making of broadcast journalism and the BBC, bad blood ensued between Churchill, supporting Baldwin, who regarded the BBC as another arm of government, and Reith, who, jealously guarding his independence, kept Winston off the airwaves during his Wilderness Years. In 1942 Churchill magnanimously gave him a peerage, and while his organisation confirmed its role of political neutrality, it was one coupled with patriotism in time of war.

The drama also taught Churchill the value of broadcast radio in times of national stress, while his *British Gazette* venture revealed to him the advantages of impartial wireless reporting being underwritten by government propaganda to shore up morale. All of these lessons encouraged Churchill to impose his will on the Ministry of Information in 1940. After the strike, a Labour MP quizzed the Chancellor on the subject of who should pay for a government newspaper should such widespread industrial action occur in future. Quick as a flash, Churchill responded: 'Make your minds perfectly clear that if ever you let loose upon us again a general strike, we will loose upon you another *British Gazette*.' The laughter on all sides at the exchange helped defuse some of the lingering tension over the recent events.

Churchill's five Budgets were criticised then (as they are today) for favouring Conservative-voting financiers and salaried classes at the expense of blue-collar workers, manufacturers and exporters, who were already under pressure from rising import competition. Paradoxically, some of the expenditure decisions he made as Chancellor initiated the defence cuts which would frustrate him throughout the 1930s. However, he soon found fate had other plans, when his term as Chancellor and in Cabinet came to an abrupt end with the general election of 30 May 1929. The Conservatives were beaten into second place with 261 seats, against Labour's 287, while the Liberals won just fifty-nine. Churchill, now under the Conservative banner, retained Epping, though his majority was halved.

Working-class support for Ramsay MacDonald and his Labour Party had trumped Baldwin's middle-class electorate, and exploited Lloyd George's Liberal legacy of distrust and broken post-war pledges of 'homes fit for heroes'. This was the first general election which embraced suffrage for all male and female adults over twenty-one. Many of the new generation of independently minded voters opted for Labour, content to ignore their parents' traditional allegiances. MacDonald would govern between 1929 and 1931, before heading a National Government. In 1935, he would relinquish the premiership back to Baldwin, who continued for two years, until he was succeeded by Neville Chamberlain (1869–1940). The latter had little affection for Churchill, until he needed him in 1939. Thus, although remaining as an MP, Winston was out of ministerial office for the next ten years.

CHAPTER 5

While England Slept

WHILE he juggled the nation's finances, Winston was rather less successful at managing his own. In September 1922 a legacy enabled him to spend £5,000 on buying the run-down house and eighty-acre estate of Chartwell, near Westerham in Kent. The proceeds from hundreds of magazine and newspaper articles (sixty-four in 1937 alone) and his next books, including six volumes of *The World Crisis* (1923–31), *My Early Life* (1930), *Thoughts and Adventures* (twenty-three essays on a wide range of topics, published in 1932), the 779,000-word *Marlborough: His Life and Times* (four volumes, 1933–38), *Great Contemporaries* (twenty-one pen portraits published in 1937, with four more added to the 1939 edition), *Arms and the Covenant* (his 1923–38 speeches, published in 1938) and *Step by Step* (collected newspaper articles from 1936–39), funded the extensive renovations on which he embarked, supplemented by his own bricklaying and pond-building efforts, with which his many visitors were expected to help. Much of his four-volume *A*

History of the English-Speaking Peoples was also completed at this time, but war and premiership intervened, and they were not edited or published until 1956–58. Churchill was initially inspired to write in the absence of a private income. Soon, however, finding he could generate 'clean' copy, to length and on time, and represented by dynamic agents, he became a prolific and instinctive penman, and we are far the richer for it – between the ages of eight and twelve, this author was obliged at school to study *My Early Life* as the model of how to write superior English.*

Interspersed with daubing colour on canvas – 'Happy are the painters for they shall not be lonely,' he wrote, adding: 'Light and colour, peace and hope, will keep them company to the end, or almost to the end, of the day' – and working at a rate of 200 bricks and 2,000 words per diem, Churchill spent his not inconsiderable income from writing (he was one of the highest-paid authors of his day, an ink-millionaire by today's standards) on structural alterations and entertaining, always spending at a slightly faster rate than he could earn. Winston's daily routine illustrates where some of it went. After bathing, splashing himself liberally with Penhaligon's not inexpensive, citrusy 'Blenheim Bouquet' (what else?) cologne, and breakfasting alone on bacon and eggs or cold lobster in his bedroom, he worked his way through each of the day's newspapers, correspondence and parliamentary

---

* Winston's output in books alone exceeded 13 million words, including 5.2 million in his many volumes of speeches. His *Second World War* contained 1.6 million; there were another 824,000 in *The World Crisis*, while the *English Speaking Peoples* came in at 510,000. For comparison, this modest biography amounts to 50,000 words.

documents until lunchtime, a heavily diluted whisky and cigar always at his side. He smoked up to ten a day, one of his valets noting that in two days his master had consumed the equivalent of a valet's weekly salary, and owned a favourite silver ashtray, which travelled everywhere with him in its own custom-made case. Churchill enjoyed a bottle of Pol Roger served in a silver tankard with his midday meal; dinner was accompanied by vintage claret or hock, with port or aged Hine (cognac) and soda, and a cigar afterwards. During the First World War, he was accused of being unpatriotic in continuing to drink German hock. 'I'm not drinking it, I'm interning it,' was his razor-sharp justification. Favourite menus included consommé, *sole Champeaux* and *tournedos Montpensier* (beef tenderloins with foie gras and black truffles), followed by Stilton and Swiss Gruyère cheese.

Out of office for a decade, he was caught and held by Chartwell. Although a money pit, the house became Churchill's island, his Albion, where he gathered his family close to his bosom. As he wrote to his wife in 1935: 'Time passes swiftly, but is it not joyous to see how great and growing is the treasure we have gathered together, amid the storms and stresses of so many eventful, and to millions tragic and terrible, years?' Mary Churchill thought Clemmie 'worked like a Trojan to make it the home and haven for us all he dreamed of', but she never loved Chartwell as did Winston. Clemmie's housekeeping of nine indoor staff, including their legendary cook Mrs Landemare, who stayed for fifteen years, three gardeners and a chauffeur (driving a car was not in Churchill's nature), plus nannies, kept the show on the road, just. There were constant mutterings about having to sell up, for the simple fact was Winston had become skilled in living just beyond his means. A note in the Churchill archives from November 1938 shows his gunsmith, James Woodward & Son, had to write asking for settlement of an account of £37 13s. which dated back to 1935 – three years overdue. Winston incurred further expense with his platoon of private secretaries and research assistants engaged in the twin production lines of historical writing and research on rearmament. Like soldiering, Churchill sensed generating millions of words of prose was tattooed deep into his DNA, reflecting: 'Writing a book is an adventure. To begin with it is a toy, an amusement; then it becomes a mistress, and then a master and then a tyrant.'

Chartwell was almost a self-contained village, with its heated outdoor swimming pool, ponds stocked with goldfish (which would also accommodate Harrods' shoal when they were obliged to close during the war), beehives, orchard and rose garden, lakes over which black swans glided, butterfly room and painting pavilion, eighteen bedrooms, eight bathrooms and nine reception rooms. The cigar storage room held between 3,000 and 4,000 cigars in humidors, mostly *Romeo y Julieta* and *La Aroma de Cuba* brands, ordered from James J. Fox of St James's. Chartwell was also equipped with a gunroom for Winston's substantial armoury of three shotguns, seven rifles, four sub-machine guns and ten pistols.

Although Churchill revelled in the thrill of the chase, hunting big game in Africa and wild boar in France, frequently quoting (in fact, slightly misquoting) the writer R. S. Surtees: 'Fox hunting provided all the glory of war with only 33 per cent of its danger,' at Chartwell he surrounded himself with a menagerie of pets. These included adopted foxes, the budgerigar Toby, bulldog Dodo, brown poodle Rufus, cats Mickey and Tango, and Nelson, his London feline, who moved from the Admiralty to Downing Street with him, and would chase away Chamberlain's cat, Bob, otherwise known as the 'Munich Mouser'.

Rufus was his closest companion and would sail with him to meet President Roosevelt in August 1941. However, Churchill banished the poodle from the Cabinet Room with the following admonition: 'No, Rufus, I haven't found it necessary to ask you to join the wartime Cabinet.' Outside there were his prize cows, pigs and butterflies, giving his life overtones of his contemporary and fellow great writing machine, P. G. Wodehouse. The two may have known one another through John Wodehouse, a Liberal MP and later 3rd Earl of Kimberley, kinsman of the comedic writer and unpaid assistant private secretary to Winston when Colonial Secretary in 1921–22. John Wodehouse appears to have helped Churchill in Leicester West during his 1923 campaign, for photographs exist of the two of them there together. We are left wondering if Churchill was an inspiration for the rose garden- and pig-loving Clarence Threepwood, 9th Earl of Emsworth, at home in his butterfly- and cattle-strewn fictional estate of Blandings Castle.*

Winston was at one with the life lived by his father, Lord Randolph. At Blenheim, twenty gamekeepers wearing brown

---

* Both Churchill and P. G. Wodehouse wrote brief pieces in *The Legion Book* (1929), published in aid of the British Legion. It contained thirty-three articles, stories and poems by leading writers of the day.

breeches and green velvet coats decorated with Marlborough-crested brass buttons had run ducal field sports with military precision. Its stable block, packed with carriage horses and fine hunters, had been overseen by a garrison of grooms, while squadrons of indoor servants kept the big house under control, with its 'moving carpet of King Charles spaniels'. Initially at Blenheim, and later at Sandhurst, in the army and in his own houses, Winston Churchill's life was one of closeness to the animal kingdom. His relationships with these mute friends, who were unquestioningly obedient, was symbiotic – in exchange for his affection, they provided a release for the huge stresses to which he subjected himself. His family saw this, Mary Churchill referring to her home as 'this happy zoo, Chartwell'. Sentimental to an extreme, in reply to Clemmie's impatience when he hesitated over the carving of a large chicken on the dining table, Winston blurted out: 'I'm just wondering if this is Ethel.'

The house, with its stunning views over the Kentish Weald, was a refuge, his own Blenheim, where he could retreat in self-imposed exile from London, and enjoy good living on his own terms. It grounded him in the past and inspired his penmanship. A visit is vital to understanding the man, for at its heart is his book-lined writing room, known as the study, where the wordsmith's enterprise and imagination generated the ocean of English required to keep the Churchills in the style to which Winston felt they should be accustomed.

Wandering the rooms today, it is not difficult to imagine the trail of cigar smoke, chaos of wine glasses, tumble of budgerigars, pet foxes, cats and dogs, and papers stained with black-cherry jam (never marmalade), as the great man paraded through his mansion, wrapped in his favourite Chinese-silk dressing gown, on which crimson-and-gold dragons chased one another around his portly frame. He worked at a specially made desk, standing up, as had his father, and came to realise his magnificent prose was as much about Britain's present and future potential as it was about recording the past progression of the English-speaking peoples, his great contemporaries or the days of Marlborough's wars. In January 1928, James Lees-Milne stayed as a guest of Churchill's son Randolph and described an evening after dinner.

> We remained at that round table till after midnight. Mr Churchill spent a blissful two hours demonstrating with decanters and wine glasses how the Battle of Jutland was fought. He got worked up like a schoolboy, making barking noises in imitation of gunfire, and blowing cigar smoke across the battle scene in imitation of gun smoke.

Chartwell also became the centre of an informal shadow government, a Kentish Westminster, where Churchill's friends and counsellors shared information and devised policies to be proclaimed in Parliament or the media. The visitors' book was opened in April 1924, and, as the house's curator Katherine Carter points out, sheds light on 'their life away from the public eye. It is the single most important record of the private life of the Churchills, charting the presence in 224 pages, via 2,316 signatures, of 780 different guests across forty years.' Invitations were eagerly sought to Winston and Clemmie's great freethinking salon, with entries including figures from every walk of life, from Max Beaverbrook, Charlie Chaplin, T. E. Lawrence (who would arrive by motorcycle and dress for dinner in Arabian robes), Albert Einstein, Walter Sickert and Violet Bonham Carter to Christabel Pankhurst, Diana Mitford, Vivien Leigh, Laurence Olivier, Generals Alexander, Freyberg and Montgomery, and President Truman – not to mention the occasional royal personage. Some deliberately omitted to sign, including Group Captain Lachlan MacLean and Wing Commander Tor Anderson, who came to confide in Churchill their concerns about the country's inadequate aerial strength; Fabian von Schlabrendorff and Major Ewald von Kleist, anti-Nazi Germans warning of the aggressiveness of the pre-war Reich; French ex-Prime Minister Léon Blum; former German chancellor Heinrich Brüning; and Desmond Morton, one of Churchill's prime sources of information regarding government unpreparedness during the 1930s.

Yet, there were those who were suspicious of the 'Chartwell set'. Stanley Baldwin, who had given Churchill the opportunity to wear his father's Chancellor's robes in 1924, was one. Although a fellow Old Harrovian, everything about his demeanour, from his pipe to his iron-and-steel, Black Country background, screamed class inferiority to Churchill's cigar-chomping, laid-back, Riviera-polo-and-country-house lifestyle. Jealousy oozed from every pore in Baldwin's contemporary criticism, shared by many:

> When Winston was born lots of fairies swooped down on his cradle with gifts – imagination, eloquence, industry and ability; and then came a fairy who said, 'No one person has a right to so many gifts,' picked him up and

75

gave him such a shake and twist that with all these gifts
he was denied judgment and wisdom.

Throughout this period, Churchill was an implacable opponent of any notion of the dismantlement of empire, from
the Government of India Act of 1935, which granted that
country a degree of autonomy, to the advent of full-blown
independence, delayed by war, in 1947. It was one of his
blind spots, something everyone but Winston could see
was on the cards, a failing some historians, such as John
Charmley, have interpreted as extreme personal racism.
He has argued, alongside numerous Indian scholars, that
Churchill saw Britain's empire as a natural consequence of
social Darwinism, with a pecking order of English-speaking
white Protestants at the top, followed by Catholics, Indians
and finally black Africans.

Based on Winston's own time in India during 1896–97,
others counter that while he may have condoned the popular
belief in the superiority of the white races (a commonly held
view of the era), he did not endorse inhumane treatment
towards non-white individuals. However, in January 1931,
when the viceroy (Lord Irwin, the future Viscount Halifax
and Churchill's rival for the premiership in 1940) released
Mahatma Gandhi from jail to take part in talks about India's
future, Churchill's usual generosity of spirit was curiously
compromised. His uncharacteristic words of 1931 are still
fed into the anti-Churchillian machine gun on a regular basis:
'It is alarming and nauseating to see Mr Gandhi, a seditious
Middle Temple lawyer, now posing as a fakir of a type well
known in the East, striding half naked to parley on equal

terms with the representative of the Emperor-King.' Such criticism is all the more abhorrent for Winston would have been aware, from his own war reporting and service, that the pacifist Gandhi had nobly led a detachment of stretcher-bearers in 1900, and displayed personal bravery at the Battle of Spion Kop when carrying wounded British soldiers from the front for several miles to a field hospital, thus receiving the Queen's South Africa Medal.

Yet Winston had been as embarrassed and angry as anyone over Brigadier Reginald Dyer's suppression of a non-existent 'uprising' in Amritsar (in the Punjab region) which killed at least 379 people and injured over a thousand more on 13 April 1919. Dyer, who had studied and imitated the suppression of the Easter Rising of 1916 in Dublin, was immediately removed from office and could never understand what he had done wrong. He was hit with a commission of inquiry and the desire of Churchill, his political overlord as Secretary of State for War, to see him disciplined, though the army demurred.

Churchill's view then was: 'Britain neither could nor should rule India by force alone'; however, it was a viewpoint he had reversed by 1935. Dyer's actions of 1919, but also Winston's words of 1931, certainly excited the desire for home rule, but would not prevent 2.5 million Indian Army soldiers in twenty-eight divisions, 30,000 Royal Indian Navy sailors in 165 vessels and 25,000 Royal Indian Air Force personnel in twelve squadrons from volunteering to fight Italians and Germans around the Mediterranean, or countering the Japanese in Malaya, Singapore, Borneo and Burma, when Churchill appealed for their help.

In a way, this decade ensconced at Chartwell almost forms part of Churchill's premiership, for without his warnings about German and Italian rearmament, as he travelled not just around the country but around the world, orating and gaining a profile which would be much needed from 1939 onwards, he would not have reached Downing Street in 1940, or become the country's most recognisable politician even before he took office again. His experience at the Ministry of Munitions and later as Minister for War and Air heightened his understanding of aviation's importance in warfare, which made him acutely sensitive to the emerging German air force, forbidden under the terms of the Versailles Treaty, but publicly unveiled in 1935. With access to secret papers and studies, brought to Chartwell by friends and admirers, Churchill was able to argue the Luftwaffe would be 50 per cent stronger than the RAF by the end of 1936 and nearly twice as strong in 1937.

The key players here were civil servants Sir Robert Vansittart (1881–1957), Permanent Undersecretary at the Foreign Office, his deputy Ralph Wigram (1890–1936) and Major Desmond Morton (1891–1971), the latter an ex-officer on Haig's staff, assigned to look after the Minister of Munitions whenever he visited the front. In 1924, Churchill transferred Morton to the Committee of Imperial Defence, responsible for intelligence on the military capabilities of other countries. Living a mile from Chartwell, during the 1930s he would walk across the fields to leak documents and sensitive information to Winston. As Richard Holmes intuitively notes, the fact Morton 'was not sacked is sufficient proof he had political clearance'. He argues: 'All three Prime

Ministers during the 1930s wanted Churchill to be as well informed as they were on the subject of German rearmament, desiring him to beat the warning drum when they could not.' Wigram was an occasional weekend guest at Chartwell, while Churchill also visited Wigram's London home. Both were part of a network of about twenty well-placed friends and sympathisers who kept Winston up to date with military developments in Britain, Germany, Italy and France.

In addition to demanding emergency acceleration of aircraft production, to which the government reluctantly acceded, Churchill pressed for research into air defence. The country had been reliant on the volunteer Royal Observer Corps (ROC) for the detection of aircraft over Great Britain since October 1925, but in December 1935 the Treasury woke up and granted £60,000 for a five-station 'Chain Home' radar network, covering approaches to the Thames Estuary, while the first Spitfire flew on 5 March 1936. Based on his experience of 1917, Churchill also proposed a Ministry of Supply to prepare Britain's industry for wartime production, but, beset with the problem of unemployment and the Great Depression, Baldwin and Chamberlain (Chancellor during 1931–37) could not envisage the provocation of placing British industry back on a wartime footing, much less how to pay for it.

Churchill was not panicked by Baldwin's unwise address to the Commons of 10 November 1932 – in which he stated: 'I think it is well also for the man in the street to realise that there is no power on earth that can protect him from being bombed. Whatever people may tell him, the bomber will always get through' – and equally sanguine about the debate held at the Oxford Union on 9 February 1933. The motion presented, 'This House will under no circumstances fight for its King and country', was passed, with 275 votes for and 153 against. Not being a university man, Winston disregarded it as an unhelpful and irrelevant undergraduate excess, though newspapermen at the time embarked on a spree of unpatriotic nonsense.

Already, the year before, Churchill had warned:

> A terrible process is astir. Germany is arming... All these bands of sturdy Teutonic youths, marching along the streets and roads of Germany, with the light in their eyes of desire to suffer for their Fatherland, are not looking for status. They are looking for weapons, and, when they have the weapons, believe me they will then ask for the return, the restoration of lost territories and lost colonies.

This was a result of his research trip to Bavaria to study the battlefield of Blenheim, when intermediaries had also tried to arrange a meeting between Churchill and Hitler in Munich. It didn't take place, of course, but had it done so, it would likely have been more akin to Anthony Eden's encounter with the Führer in March 1935 – when, on finding they had been stationed opposite one another in the trenches, the two men refought First World War battles on the backs of menu cards – than to Chamberlain's stiff and awkward performance in 1938.

One comrade on the Bavarian tour was Churchill's good friend, the brilliant Oxford don Professor Frederick Lindemann (1886–1957), who was of German extraction but pathologically anti-Nazi, and known to all as 'the Prof'.

Their friendship had begun in 1921, when Winston was drawn to his ability of explaining all manner of scientific issues concisely, and later by their shared concerns about the danger posed by Hitler and the pre-war inadequacy of British air defence. Winston opined Lindemann's brain was a 'beautiful piece of mechanism', and one admirer observed: 'He would write a memorandum on high strategy one day, and a thesis on egg production on the next.' Teetotal and a vegetarian, Lindemann would become by far the most prominent guest at Chartwell (signing the visitor's book on eighty-six occasions), and was later raised to the peerage in 1941 as Lord Cherwell with a seat in the Cabinet, to act as the Prime Minister's principal scientific advisor.

Another close member of Churchill's political staff and travelling companion was his Parliamentary Private Secretary from 1926 to 1929, Robert Boothby (1900–86). He met Hitler in 1932, seeing the 'unmistakable glint of madness in his eyes', which persuaded him to join Winston's (then) lonely band of parliamentary campaigners for faster rearmament. Another ardent rearmer was MP Major Ronald Cartland (1907–40), who also visited pre-war Germany, finding its treatment of Jews appalling. He might have featured as a future minister under Churchill, had he not been killed at Dunkirk, and was mourned ever after by his sister, the writer Dame Barbara. Also hugely important was the controversial Irishman Brendan Bracken (1901–58). Of obscure origins, he managed Winston's pre-war election campaigns, rose to found both the *Financial Times* and *The Banker* magazine, acquired a half-share in *The Economist*, became an MP in 1929, was Parliamentary Private Secretary when his master was at the Admiralty, and was also used by Evelyn Waugh as a model for Rex Mottram in *Brideshead Revisited*. The Bracken residence at 8 Lord North Street became Churchill's interwar anti-appeasement base in London. Labelled by Baldwin as 'Winston's faithful *chela*' (Hindustani for disciple), Bracken, who is desperately in need of a new biography, was Churchill's sounding board, gatekeeper, adjutant and spin doctor throughout 1929–39. His proximity and influence were resented particularly by Clemmie and Randolph, but he would encourage Winston to contest the premiership against Halifax in May 1940, and later emerged as the highly successful wartime Minister for Information.

Then came the abdication crisis of December 1936, with Baldwin and much of Britain's ruling class unwilling to accept the American divorcée Wallis Simpson as the new King's consort, and Edward VIII's refusal to give her up. He would be succeeded by his brother Bertie, who became George VI. Edward was given the title of Duke of Windsor and styled 'His Royal Highness' following his abdication, and married Simpson the following year. In an appalling lapse of judgement, Churchill had initially supported Edward VIII through blind loyalty to the Crown, but soon remarked to Clemmie: 'You were right. I see now the "other one" [meaning Edward] wouldn't have done.'

Shortly after, he wrote to the exiled duke, warning: 'There is a great deal of bitterness from those who are hostile to you, and from those who are hostile because of their disappointment [in your decision]. The line I take is "I wish to see the King reign gloriously, and the Duke of Windsor live happily"' – but he did not dwell on the incompatibility of the two desires. Churchill had been slow to realise the personal weakness of Edward VIII and the compelling strength of his future bride. Historians Andrew Lownie and Alexander Larman have separately observed both Baldwin and Chamberlain were aware Wallis was passing state secrets to German intelligence, while Edward VIII also expressed sympathy for the Nazi regime, culminating in the couple's visit to Germany of 11–23 October 1937. They met several leading Nazis, including Hess, Goebbels and Göring, and conferred with Hitler in his mountain lair at Berchtesgaden, but weren't the only ones to have fallen under the Führer's spell.

Churchill's old friend David Lloyd George had met Hitler a year earlier, in September 1936, afterwards writing in the *Daily Express*:

> He is a born leader of men. A magnetic and dynamic personality with a single-minded purpose, a resolute will and a dauntless heart. He is not merely in name but in fact the national Leader... Catholic and Protestant, Prussian and Bavarian, employer and workman, rich and poor, have been consolidated into one people. Religious, provincial and class origins no longer divide the nation... I have never met a happier people than the Germans, and Hitler is one of the greatest of men.

Unless one was Jewish, of course. Lloyd George had let the wool be pulled over his eyes in the same way others visiting the Soviet Union at this time had done so wearing rose-tinted spectacles. His view of Germany was not uncommon among influential Britons, who saw only what they wanted to see, but within three years were wishing they could reverse the clock and eat their words. Others (labelled by Churchill as the 'Heil Hitler brigade in London society') were more extreme, pro-fascist and -appeasement and anti-Semitic, not least Sir Oswald Mosley, his wife Diana and her sister Unity Mitford; their father the 2nd Lord Redesdale; Lord Tavistock (later 12th Duke of Bedford); Viscount Rothermere, owner of the *Daily Mail* and *Daily Mirror*; Admiral Sir Barry Domvile; military theorist Major General J. F. C. Fuller; John Amery, son of Winston's fellow MP and friend Leo; the best-selling author of *Tarka the Otter*, Henry Williamson; and members of the 'Right Club', led by the MP Captain Archibald Maule Ramsay. Many would be interned during the war.

Throughout his life, the East European Bear in all its forms was a bogeyman for Churchill. He had been brought up to understand that the Russia of the tsars threatened British interests in India and the balance of power in the Middle East. But its replacement, the Communism of Lenin and Stalin, alarmed him more – partly because their brand of social revolution threatened the class into which he had been born, and had toppled a monarchy. However nastily absolute, hereditary crowns were a concept he believed valid for governing much of the planet. Fundamentally, he saw the dictatorship of the Reds in Moscow as undermining every freedom of expression and democracy Europe had once known, or might attain. The Lenin and Trotsky doctrine of worldwide revolution spread by political violence only served to confirm all his prejudices and, even in the 1930s, he took every opportunity to warn of the Soviet Union's long-term threat to world order, not least the flow of Middle Eastern oil.

Churchill's background as a soldier and the several governmental portfolios he had held, which had brought him insight into military and foreign affairs, naturally led him to view the rise of Hitler with even greater concern. Though Chamberlain had returned from Munich in September 1938 in the belief he had averted war with Germany and had achieved 'peace for our time', a phrase borrowed from the Book of Common Prayer, Churchill saw it differently. On 5 October 1938, during the third day of the Commons debate on Munich, whose famous document, surrendering the Czech Sudetenland to Nazi Germany, had been signed five days earlier, Churchill called the accord 'a total and unmitigated defeat'. Having disclaimed any personal animosity towards Chamberlain, he spoke for an hour to criticise the agreement and more generally the policy of appeasement, arguing the rest of Czechoslovakia would be 'engulfed in the Nazi regime... The maintenance of peace depends upon the accumulation of deterrents against the aggressor'.

It is noticeable how many of Chamberlain's supporters, including the man himself, had not fought in 1914–18, and were opposed to war in any shape or form, whereas those who had combat experience, including Churchill, Anthony Eden (1897–1977) and rising star Harold Macmillan (1894–1986), with mud on their boots from the trenches, were less afraid of another war and argued for rearmament. In his speech, Winston compared Chamberlain's governance with the Saxon king Ethelred the Unready, and invoked the biblical book of Daniel to declare: 'We have sustained a defeat without a war... Thou art weighed in the balance and found wanting.'

He concluded:

Do not suppose this is the end. This is only the beginning of the reckoning. This is only the first sip, the first foretaste of a bitter cup which will be proffered to us year by year unless by a supreme recovery of moral health and martial vigour, we arise again and take our stand for freedom as in the olden time.

Churchill would use these phrases again in his wartime oratory and books, and biographer Roy Jenkins thought it 'a speech of power and intransigence', but the Commons voted 366 to 144 to support the government. Winston and his supporters chose to abstain. His words had little immediate effect outside Westminster, though there was a move to unseat him in Epping, where he braved a motion of no confidence, winning by 100 votes to forty-four.

Other Britons, such as the popular writer and distinguished airship and aircraft designer Nevil Shute, were able to see the direction of world events from a professional point of view. Hastened by the Munich crisis, he published his fifth novel, *What Happened to the Corbetts*, in February 1939. It chronicles the fictional life of solicitor Peter Corbett and his family when their neighbourhood in Southampton is suddenly blitzed by bomber fleets belonging to an unnamed power (obviously Germany). Cities across southern England are reduced to helplessness under the bombs; typhoid and cholera break out as the inhabitants flee – but, after many trials, the Corbetts manage to reach safety in their small yacht.

Shute's volume hit the bookshops at just the right moment to become a bestseller in a Britain suddenly panicked by the threat of aerial destruction. In particular, it put the wind up the nation's ill-prepared Air Raid Precautions service, to whom free copies were presented by the publisher. Yet Shute misread the tea leaves, and the ruination he predicted for Britain never came to pass. As he later observed, he overstressed the effects of blast and poison gas but severely underestimated the potential of fire in aerial bombing. The inhabitants of Berlin, Cologne and Dresden would not disagree.

Britons clung to Chamberlain's promises of peace, which were rudely abused the following month by the anti-Jewish violence across Germany of 9–10 November 1938, Kristallnacht, and then on 15 March 1939, when the Reich overran the rest of the Czech nation, something Churchill had predicted in his speech. Chamberlain countered first by doubling the size of Britain's reserve force, the Territorial Army. He made this statement to the Commons on 29 March 1939 without reference to the War Office or anybody else, naively expecting his words alone would steady the nation and make Hitler think again. In obliging the regular army to help expand reservist units, Chamberlain's words actually hindered rather than helped rearmament. On 27 April 1939, he doubled down on his error by insisting his Secretary of State for War, Leslie Hore-Belisha, announce limited conscription for single men aged between twenty and twenty-two. Neither step remotely deterred Germany, and inadvertently slowed down Britain's preparations for any war, by forcing the regulars to cease preparations for battle and attend to training their reservist and conscript chums. Conflict was on the horizon, galloping fast towards Western Europe, threatening to sweep all before it.

Though out of office, Churchill had a behind-the-scenes hand in George VI's state visit to Canada and the United States of May–June 1939, the first of a British sovereign to the latter country. The King and Queen immediately saw eye to eye with the Roosevelts, with George fighting his disabling stammer, Franklin his polio. The President was former Assistant Secretary of the Navy (1913–20); the King had served on the battleship *Collingwood* at Jutland. The visit was a huge success and, in terms of forging Anglo-American relations, vital to the war about to transpire. The *Daily Mail* opined their return to Albion's shores was 'the greatest of all homecomings, the closing scene of the greatest royal day since the Coronation'. The new King had outclassed Chamberlain at Munich and outsmarted anything his older brother might have achieved in his talks with Hitler at Berchtesgaden.

Back in December 1931, Churchill had been struck by a car in New York City, underlining less that he was accident-prone (incredibly so), but more he was almost unique among British politicians in regularly crossing the Atlantic. By 1939 he had learned how to run many government departments and built a network of zealous admirers who were prepared to risk their positions to pass vital intelligence and information to him. While 'horizon-scanning' and strategic studies are common disciplines today, few British politicians had the curiosity to trouble themselves with such matters in the 1930s. Having in his twenties foreseen the roar and rattle of the machine age, in *Thoughts and Adventures* (1932), he had written:

High authorities tell us that new sources of power, vastly more important than any we yet know, will surely be discovered. Nuclear energy is incomparably greater than the molecular energy which we use today... There is no question among scientists that this gigantic source of energy exists. What is lacking is the match to set the bonfire alight, or it may be the detonator to cause the dynamite to explode. The scientists are looking for this.

On 4 May 1939, he predicted in the *Daily Telegraph* a 'new outrage or invasion by Hitler, most likely against Poland'. By July, Churchill was forecasting an alliance between Germany and Russia. He was right: a Nazi–Soviet Pact was signed in Moscow a month later, on 23 August. This 'other piece of paper' contained a secret clause allowing a Russo-German partition of Poland, and was designed to allay Soviet fears that when (not if) the Wehrmacht stormed across the Polish border, the aggression would be directed at Stalin. Seven years hence, on 5 March 1946, Churchill would make a famous speech about the advent of the Cold War, at Fulton, Missouri. It contained this profound reflection on the appeasement era: 'There never was a war in all history easier to prevent by timely action than the one which has just desolated such great areas of the globe. It could have been prevented in my belief without the firing of a single shot.'

Tory MP and biographer Robert Rhodes James argued the life of Churchill – admired for his drive and brilliance but distrusted for his supposed lack of judgement – had been a failure to 1939. Yet it is equally possible to contend the opposite. Winston's so-called 'Wilderness Years' did not represent a decade out of power at all. He had remained influential, a raincloud over successive governments, but discreetly in touch with them. Furthermore, the cards for supreme leadership could not have fallen in Churchill's favour had he absented himself from his 'Chartwell set', instead lurking in Whitehall, holding senior office in pro-appeasement administrations. However, the moment for which he felt destined, for which almost every aspect of his life had prepared him, was about to unfold.

PART II

Winston Churchill at Downing Street on his 80th birthday, 30th November 1954: the man and his props, chief of which was his wife Clementine, without whom he could not have managed his extraordinary life.

CHAPTER 6

Twilight War

E VEN after Hitler's panzers clattered into Poland at 4.45 a.m. on Friday, 1 September 1939, the profoundly pacifist Chamberlain was reluctant to initiate a second struggle against Germany. Although Poland had formed a defensive military alliance with Britain and France on 31 March 1939, it turned out neither country had the political will or the military ability to intervene, something Hitler had foreseen. Chamberlain was faced with German aggression he hoped would not happen and could do nothing about. He rather wished the inconvenience of Germany's challenge to Britain's military guarantee would just go away. It would not, and, over the weekend of 2–3 September, he prevaricated, before the Cabinet decided collectively to coerce him into making a stand. Accordingly, first thing on Sunday morning, his namesake and ambassador in Berlin, Neville Henderson, was instructed to hand Hitler's foreign ministry an ultimatum demanding a withdrawal from Poland. Receiving no response, at 11.15 a.m. Chamberlain made his fateful announcement to the nation of the second war against Germany within the lifetimes of many.

Many never heard the now-famous broadcast, being in the midst of prayer in churches and chapels throughout the land, and it was left to their priests and ministers to give form to Chamberlain's words, often tacked on to the end of the morning sermon. In London, air-raid sirens sounded, as though German aircraft had been circling in wait. It was a false alarm, but underlined the new-found tensions of the moment. From their London house at 11 Morpeth Mansions, SW1, Churchill, armed with 'a bottle of brandy and other appropriate comforts', descended to an air-raid shelter with Clemmie: 'Everyone was cheerful and jocular, as is the English manner when about to encounter the unknown,' he later wrote. He had not been at prayer, but was eagerly awaiting Chamberlain's communication, as he had been ever since the occupation of the Czech lands that spring. Memoirs indicate how Chartwell had become an unofficial command centre, festooned with maps, military papers and rows of coloured telephones, with Winston's secretaries and research assistants repurposed from history to current affairs, taking notes and offering ideas for all manner of European and imperial strat- agems, presided over by their reanimated master.

Chartwell's frequent callers now wore the dark blue of the Royal Navy, the lighter shade of Air Force blue or army khaki. All had a spring in their step. All were convinced battle loomed. Only on 3 September did Chamberlain real- ise he could no longer avoid summoning the nation's most famous warlord back into government and recalled Winston to his old post at the Admiralty, while he made his Prime

Ministerial proclamation against Germany. Cold, austere, aloof and lacking the common touch, Chamberlain couldn't quite grasp his descent from saviour-of-the-nation status at Munich, a year earlier, to pariah for having misread Hitler so badly. And now he had to turn to the ebullient and popular Churchill, who, it turned out, had been right about Germany all along. We are left with a pervading sense of Chamberlain's recruitment of Churchill back into the Cabinet being nearly as much a personal defeat as going to war with Hitler.

With almost the slickness of a cinematic screenplay, as the new First Lord of the Admiralty later recorded, the Navy Board 'were kind enough to signal the Fleet, "Winston is back." So it was that I came again to the room I had quitted in pain and sorrow almost exactly a quarter of a century before.' The pleasing signal was also reflected in newspaper headlines: the surname 'Churchill' was not needed. He was the country's best-known politician, a 'brand' in modern terminology. The news indicated, not only to the Royal Navy but to the nation, Britain was again in safer hands. According to contemporary opinion polls, though, some expected the much younger Anthony Eden to be summoned. He had fought on the Western Front, and was awarded a Military Cross for bravery in 1916, the same year becoming the youngest adjutant at the front, aged just nineteen. A glittering post-war political career followed, which saw him sent twice to dine with Hitler in 1935, subsequently becoming Baldwin's Foreign Secretary in December of the same year. However, he resigned in February 1938 over Chamberlain's appeasement of Mussolini, going on to lead a parliamentary gang of

Tory dissenters. As Eden later wrote, the term 'appeasement' originally meant to 'settle strife'. Only after Munich did it come to represent a craven foreign policy.*

Instead of being sent to the more aggressive Admiralty, Eden became Chamberlain's Secretary of State for Dominion Affairs, and in December 1940 would return to his old job, becoming Churchill's second Foreign Secretary. His time at the helm would come later. Almost more important for Winston in 1939 was the congratulatory message received on 11 September from the man who had been the former assistant secretary of the US Navy during the First World War (and therefore Churchill's near counterpart as First Lord of the Admiralty). The pair had first met on 29 July 1918, when Franklin D. Roosevelt (1882–1945) had joined an American fact-finding mission to Europe to determine how best to support Britain and France. Now President, he addressed his coded note to 'Naval Person' (which Churchill amended to 'Former Naval Person' in later correspondence, after becoming Prime Minister). It indicated the informal Churchillian network at work, which no other British politician had at their disposal, or had bothered to cultivate.

On land, an inactive *drôle de guerre* – 'phoney war' to the Allied troops assembling in France – caused by an absence of Germans to fight, meant strategy-making under Chamberlain faltered. Britain dusted off its war plans and dispatched the bulk of its regular army to France with all of its vehicles, and

* Historian Tim Bouverie observes that appeasement switched from being a reactive policy to the claims of Japan, Italy and Germany over Manchuria, Ethiopia and Austria, to a proactive one under Chamberlain, to solve the issue of Czechoslovakia.

most of the Territorials. Led by General Lord Gort, holder of a Victoria Cross, three Distinguished Service Orders and a Military Cross, the six divisions of the British Expeditionary Force (BEF) committed in two corps represented the most motorised army on the planet, with France and Germany still heavily reliant on horses. Reluctant to make any first moves on land, Chamberlain restricted Bomber Command to attacking warships, mining German harbours and dropping leaflets calling for a peaceable end to hostilities. On no account were bombs to be substituted for paper, lest the Germans retaliate.

For the first six months of the war, Bomber Command would make 262 ineffective night sorties over German ports, at a cost of thirteen aircraft, and 173 daylight raids, losing thirty-one machines. The RAF would have to wait until Churchill became premier before being authorised to hit industrial targets east of the Rhine. It was not until March 1942 and the presentation of Lindemann's 'de-housing' paper to Churchill, which advocated area bombardment of German cities in order to, by destroying their homes, break the will of the German people, that it found a strategy it could deliver. The shift in policy would coincide with the arrival in February 1942 of both a new aircraft, the Avro Lancaster, and a new chief, Air Chief Marshal Sir Arthur Harris. Meanwhile Bomber Command wrestled with poor morale among its crews caused by the unwarlike missions for which Chamberlain was risking their lives.

Only at sea was the war pursued with vigour from the first hours, which suited Churchill down to the ground. On the first night of the conflict, with lights blacked out and zigzagging her way to Canada, the civilian liner *Athenia* was torpedoed with the loss of 117 lives. Within weeks the Nazi newspaper *Völkischer Beobachter* was alleging Churchill had arranged her sinking to turn neutral opinion against Germany. There were early losses of major warships to U-boats: the carrier *Courageous* on 17 September and the battleship *Royal Oak* on 14 October, the latter at anchor in the allegedly submarine-proof anchorage of Scapa Flow in the Orkney Islands, collectively killing 1,354 navy personnel. The score was evened on 17 December, when a major German battleship, *Admiral Graf Spee*, was cornered after a ship-sinking spree in the South Atlantic. Following a gun battle off the River Plate, she put into the neutral port of Montevideo for repairs, but was later scuttled outside the harbour. In 1956, the drama would be re-enacted in a British war film, to Churchill's delight. On 21 February 1940, Churchill's victorious crews paraded through London, an event which the First Lord ensured gained maximum publicity. Much to Chamberlain's private annoyance, in the British public's mind the only warlike activity taking place was at sea, and Winston Churchill was running it.

The Admiralty scored another notable success in tracking down the *Graf Spee*'s support vessel, the tanker *Altmark*, which was carrying 299 prisoners taken from vessels sunk by the German warship. At anchor in the neutral waters of a Norwegian fjord, on 16 February 1940 *Altmark* was forcibly boarded by cutlass-waving matelots from the British destroyer *Cossack*, who liberated the captives. A huge crowd and news cameras greeted the destroyer when she landed the former prisoners at Leith, and the story made headlines across the world. The *Altmark* incident encouraged both sides to focus on military options for Norway. While the Germans planned a military invasion for 9–10 April to include Denmark, the Anglo-French alliance schemed to blockade neutral Norwegian waters and deny passage of high-grade iron ore from Sweden to Germany.

British manoeuvres began on 7–8 April, and rapidly the two armadas clashed, unaware of each other's intentions. Although losing several of its own destroyers, the British Home Fleet massacred half the entire German destroyer force in two engagements at Narvik. Much less satisfactory were Franco-British army expeditions to Narvik and Trondheim to support Norway, which though neutral was being fast overrun by German mountain and paratroops. A lack of amphibiosity, requiring troops and supplies to undergo the tedious and lengthy business of disembarkation from ordinary merchant ships by crane and derrick, under constant air attack, meant most of the predominantly British force had withdrawn by 30 April rather than risk capture.

At sea, Churchill's navy lost two cruisers, seven destroyers and a submarine, which the fleet was able to absorb, to Germany's four cruisers, ten destroyers and six U-boats, plus many more damaged, which the Reich could ill afford. Yet on land the Allied campaign had been a fiasco, one cause of the debacle being British maritime and land power operating in resolute independence from each other, which Churchill's subsequent *Second Word War* would do its best to conceal. With Norway evoking memories of Gallipoli twenty-five years earlier, Parliament immediately determined to pick over the events in a debate scheduled for 7–9 May. Chamberlain and his front bench opened with a series of unimpressive speeches, confirming the general dissatisfaction with his conduct of the war. Liberal, Labour and some Tory members accused Chamberlain, but specifically *not* Churchill, of general incompetence in military matters.

Lasting impressions were made by three Churchill supporters. First, the highly decorated Admiral Sir Roger Keyes, a Portsmouth MP and Winston's one-time polo partner at Chartwell, addressed the House in full dress uniform, beginning 'I speak for the navy' and thereafter turning his gun turrets on Chamberlain, expressing a wish to see 'proper use made of Churchill's great abilities'. He was followed later by Leo Amery (1873–1955), Churchill's exact contemporary at Harrow and MP for Birmingham Sparkbrook, who concluded an impassioned speech by quoting three memorable lines of Oliver Cromwell's: 'You have sat too long here for any good you have been doing. Depart, I say, and let us have done with you. In the name of God, go' – pointing at Chamberlain as he spoke. Finally, the seventy-seven-year-old former Prime Minister David Lloyd George castigated the government's lack of planning and preparation for Norway:

> The right honourable Gentleman spoke about the gallantry of our men, and we are all equally proud of them. It thrills us to read the stories. All the more shame that we should have made fools of them... For three or four years I thought to myself that the facts with regard to Germany were exaggerated by the First Lord of the Admiralty, but he was right. Then came the war. The tempo was hardly speeded

up. There was the same leisureliness and inefficiency. Will anybody tell me that he is satisfied with what we have done about aeroplanes, tanks, guns, especially anti-aircraft guns? Is anyone here satisfied with the steps we took to train an Army to use them? Nobody is satisfied. The whole world knows that. And here we are in the worst strategic position in which this country has ever been placed.

At this stage Churchill intervened: 'I take complete responsibility for everything that has been done by the Admiralty, and I take my full share of the burden.' Quick as a flash, Lloyd George responded with a memorable metaphor: 'The right honourable Gentleman must not allow himself to be converted into an air-raid shelter to keep the splinters from hitting his colleagues.' Then he, too, called for Chamberlain's resignation. In the ensuing vote of confidence, forty-one MPs who normally supported the government voted against, while another sixty abstained.

Many historians and politicians regard this as the greatest of all parliamentary debates, coming as it did at a time when the nation was about to face its gravest danger. Lloyd George thought it the 'most momentous in the history of Parliament', while Harold Macmillan observed it 'changed British, perhaps world history'. Current affairs commentator Andrew Marr has ventured it was 'one of the greatest parliamentary moments ever, and little about it was inevitable', while former Commons speaker Betty Boothroyd assessed that Leo Amery's speech, 'by elevating patriotism above party, showed the backbencher's power to help change the course of history'.

Chamberlain was undone. Technically he had won the

debate, but he realised he had lost the country. On 9 May, he contemplated resignation, favouring his Foreign Secretary, Halifax, as successor. The latter was not remotely warlike and one of those who had earlier opposed bombing the Reich, lest the Germans retaliate. The following morning Germany's long-planned invasion of France and the Low Countries began, forcing Chamberlain's hand. Halifax was reluctant to assume the mantle, confiding to his diary: 'Apart altogether from Churchill's qualities as compared with my own at this particular juncture, what would in fact be my position? Churchill would be running Defence... I should speedily become a more or less honorary Prime Minister, living in a kind of twilight just outside the things that really mattered.' No doubt concerned by the potential difficulties of leading the Commons in war – and rally-ing the radical socialists of the Labour Party – while having, as a peer, physically to sit in the Lords, Edward Frederick Lindley Wood, 3rd Viscount Halifax, made the best political decision of any Briton in the twentieth century, and wisely declined.*

With the Labour opposition stipulating they would join a coalition government, but never under Chamberlain, it was obvious his time had gone, and – for all Labour's traditional distrust of Churchill – the latter's time had arrived. Its 'finest hour' was upon the nation, with a new government ushered in by no great democratic mandate but by a small multiparty coterie of Westminster politicians.

Some recent writers are coming around to Chamberlain, arguing he at least bought time after Munich for Britain to

---

* Not until the 1963 Peerage Act could hereditary members of the House of Lords disclaim their peerages and sit in the House of Commons.

rearm, but this ignores how he bungled the Territorial Army and conscription measures in March–April 1939, spent much of 1–3 September trying to avoid going to war, and failed to bring Churchill back into government until the last possible moment. Robert Harris, author of the novel *Munich*, suggests the paper Chamberlain waved on returning from his meeting with the Führer was a German trap to lull him into a false sense of security. Further, he surmised Chamberlain considered the document 'a tripwire', hoping Hitler would stick to his word: 'but if he didn't, he would have the agreement Hitler had broken.' Another writer, Michael Dobbs, argues the still insecure King George VI desired his good friend Lord Halifax follow Chamberlain, with a sense of 'letting Winston try and fail as premier, ready for a Halifax–Chamberlain administration to thereafter return'.

Had he left power earlier, Chamberlain might have preserved his reputation as one of Britain's foremost social reformers, but with his legendary obstinacy refused to try to reprise his honour. In one of his last letters before death, he reiterated: 'I regret nothing that I have done and I can see nothing undone that I ought to have done,' misquoting another line from the Prayer Book. Prompt criticism surfaced in July 1940 in a small booklet, written pseudonymously by three journalists. *Guilty Men*, by 'Cato', excoriated Chamberlain's record of inadequate preparation for war and sold more than 200,000 copies, irretrievably crippling his reputation.*

---

* The next offering of Gollancz, publishers of *Guilty Men*, was the equally propagandistic *Battle: The Life Story of Winston Churchill*. By its third edition, the cover bore the tribute: 'So entertaining and romantic that I read it right through a long night raid and was oblivious to bombs and barrage.'

Identified as the leading appeaser of the pre-war period, honourable but strategically blind, Chamberlain, who was probably suffering from gout and certainly the bowel cancer which killed him on 9 November 1940, consistently misread the international picture and, limpet-like, clung to power until the very last second. Historian David Dutton opines:

> for good or ill, he will always be tied to his policy toward Germany. Whatever else may be said of Chamberlain's public life, his reputation will depend upon assessments of this moment and this policy. To expect otherwise is like hoping Pontius Pilate will one day be judged as a successful provincial administrator of the Roman Empire.

Churchill had been on the receiving end of Conservative venom and divisiveness throughout the 1930s, but developed an ability not to hold political grudges. He was collegiate, congenial and clubbable, whether in the Commons or over dinners at the Other Club, and understood he needed as united a National Government as possible. He formed a war cabinet of five, including Chamberlain and Halifax (a nod to their supporters, whom he had yet to win over) and the two Labour leaders, Clement Attlee and Arthur Greenwood. Having witnessed decades of weak leadership, Churchill's style was to run matters as decisively as possible, additionally appointing himself Leader of the House of Commons and Minister of Defence.

There was no Ministry of Defence, and this office was devised to bring him military oversight via his 'chief staff officer' (a Churchillian invention), Major General Hastings 'Pug' Ismay, as John Kiszely reminds us in his new biography. Ismay kept his master informed of the deliberations of the Chiefs of Staff Committee (comprising the navy, army and air force heads), though Churchill often attended in person. Clement Attlee (1883–1967), his deputy Prime Minister – another innovation – substituted for his master, exhaustively as it transpired, throughout and wherever needed. Attlee's modesty and innate intelligence were a perfect foil to Churchill's brash dominance, and they formed a very trusting and professional duo throughout the war. Away from the glare of Churchill's sun, modern historians, this author included, are reassessing Attlee's steady and highly professional governance of the nation's affairs, due to his instinctive decency coupled with an ability to resist politely the tutoring and mentoring of the great man.

Sensing he needed to offer a transparent alternative to Hitler's dictatorship, Churchill desired Parliament to be a vital element in the day-to-day conduct of the war. It would be the Commons to whom Churchill would report the highs and lows, and deliver his stirring speeches, not the media. For him to be able to concentrate on strategic decision-making, he needed a tame, but not docile, House. Aware Asquith had fallen from power in December 1916 as a result of domestic political intrigues, Churchill distributed power wisely, bringing in trade-union leader Ernest Bevin as Minister of Labour to guarantee the cooperation of the nation's workforce, the vital nature of which he understood from his time at the Board of Trade, Home Office and Ministry of Munitions.

He also deftly balanced responsibility for the three forces between A. V. Alexander (Labour) at the Admiralty, Anthony Eden (Conservative) at the War Office and Archibald Sinclair (Liberal) as the new Minister for Air – all ministries Winston had run in the past. Sinclair (1890–1970), leader of the Liberal Party, was another of Winston's network, having served as second in command of his 6th Royal Scots Fusiliers on the Western Front in 1915–16.

Dominating Parliament during the war years, Churchill was curiously vulnerable. Although he kept his old network of friends and informants, such as Desmond Morton, close, he had no power base – as had the Chamberlains in Birmingham, MPs from the trade unions and professional classes, or those from some of the older political dynasties in the shires – and so relied on the one weapon in his own arsenal to dominate Parliament: his oratory. The effort and polish he put into his speeches (only later issued to the BBC and print media, and rarely relayed live) underlined the respect he had for Parliament, which he would never take for granted. It also reflected Churchill's deep appreciation of British history and reverence for the nation's institutions.

On his third day in office, he addressed the Commons for the first time as its master. This was the occasion of his 'I have nothing to offer but blood, toil, tears and sweat' speech. It was a device to unify Parliament, dangerously divided only days earlier, together with a statement of the simplest of aims: victory. Here, Churchill was offering something he could not actually deliver. Strategically wise, and gifted with a sense of geopolitics incorporating both human and physical geography, he knew in 1940 his job would be to ensure Britain's survival. Victory would only be delivered later, with the assistance of Roosevelt's United States.

Churchill was aware his opposite number had first to win the 5 November 1940 presidential election, ironically fought by Roosevelt on promises of non-intervention, in order to help him. Additionally, Winston needed to undermine the still-active appeasement faction in his own party, as well as advertise to the United States that his country was united and focused, despite the scepticism of America's old-school Irish republican, and pro-isolationist ambassador, Joe Kennedy.

The message was addressed to the British Empire, too, for Churchill was relying on the manpower, shipping and huge raw-material resources the imperial partners would commit to his leadership. This was the era when cartoonist David Low published his sketch of a British soldier standing on a wave-drenched rock on the southern English coast, shaking his fist at approaching German bombers. The caption in London's *Evening Standard* – 'Very well, alone' – was a misnomer. Britain was not alone – never alone. She was but the tip of the imperial iceberg, which vastly outnumbered anything the Germans and Italians combined could bring to war, but the image helped magnify the peril Churchill understood might assault his island home. This was emphasised on the evening of 14 May, the day after the 'blood, toil, tears and sweat' speech, when Churchill directed his Secretary of State for War, Anthony Eden, to broadcast a call for volunteers to join an armed citizen militia – the Local Defence Volunteers (LDV), later renamed the Home Guard. Half a million were expected; heeding Eden's words, three times that number joined.*

---

* With great prescience Churchill had personally called for the raising of a home defence force of 500,000 as early as 8 October 1939, though no action was taken. They were stood down on 3 December 1944.

CHAPTER 7

Into Battle

MEANWHILE the Germans had skirted the French Maginot Line, whose roots lay in competing strategies espoused by Great War commanders to protect the Franco-German border against repeats of 1870 and 1914. Some generals favoured a line of continuous fortifications. The majority, led by marshals Foch and Pétain, wanted 'fortified regions' constructed as centres of resistance for later offensive action, while a minority of modernisers, of whom Colonel Charles de Gaulle was one, derided expensive fixed defences, instead advocating cheaper, more agile methods of war, involving tanks and innovative doctrine.

After many studies and staff papers the Foch–Pétain school won, and between 1930 and 1939 France blew 3 billion francs, a huge proportion of the defence budget, on a Hobbit-like network of forty-five underground forts, arranged at ten-mile intervals; ninety-seven lesser forts and 352 concrete positions, connected by narrow-gauge railways; and nearly seventy miles of tunnels, stretching from Switzerland to Luxembourg. After 1934, a weaker extension was built, reaching the Channel, but the Franco-Belgian addition proved difficult for several reasons. Chief among them were cross-frontier main roads and railway lines which could not be easily blocked; the embarrassment of fortifying a frontier shared with an ally (although in 1937 Belgium repudiated her alliances with Britain and France, and declared neutrality out of sheer terror of Nazi Germany); and the many industrial conurbations in the area, which prevented the construction of barbed-wire obstacles, trenches and anti-tank ditches.

The subterranean sprawl of cement and steel was named after André Maginot, veteran of Verdun and Minister of War from 1928 to 1932, who found the government money for the project. 'Line' was a misnomer, for it was never designed to be continuous, but to provide centres of resistance where French reserves could first assemble over several weeks, then counter-attack their foes. However, many came to believe the propaganda used to justify its expense: Maginot's shield would block any German attack. In time, his school of concrete encouraged an almost mystic defensive mentality among soldiers and civilians alike.

The Belgians also invested heavily in fixed fortifications, the principal one being Fort Ében-Émael, a Maginot copy on the Dutch–Belgian border. It lasted less than a day, being taken by *Fallschirmjäger* (parachute) and glider forces in a few hours on 10–11 May 1940. The mission would cost the Germans six killed and nineteen wounded (out of 500) for the capture of the entire citadel, plus a thousand Belgian soldiers. In protecting the coal-and-steel wealth of Alsace and Lorraine, the Maginot Line did exactly what it was intended to, which was to deflect a German army into attacking via Belgium, theoretically robbing Berlin of any possible surprise, and reflected France's need to conserve her manpower, given the disparity between their respective populations, of 39 million to Germany's 70 million.

There was one flaw in this plan, however. To save money, Maginot's designers gambled and made their shield weakest at roughly its midpoint. This was adjacent to the heavily wooded Ardennes, primarily in Belgium and Luxembourg, where military logic suggested a German army was unlikely to be able to assemble and attack in secrecy, while the region's extensive forests would fatally slow any movements of hostile armour, artillery and infantry. French war games in 1938 indicated a minimum passage time of ten days. In the event the Germans, who did attack in precisely this area, managed it in three, and in complete secrecy.

After 10 May, the French were slow to wake up to the danger in their centre, and the long columns of armour snaking over temporary bridges thrown across the Meuse. During the night of 12–13 May, Europe's largest traffic jam, stretching back sixty miles through the Ardennes and into Germany, would have made a prize target for any air force, but French attention was elsewhere. As one German exclaimed: 'We arrived at the river and waited for your aircraft to appear. The skies remained clear, so we put across our bridges. Next, we installed our anti-aircraft defences. Only then did you oblige us with attacks, and we shot you down.' In four days, the RAF lost sixty out of its 111 light bombers while hitting German bridgeheads, with the French *Armée de l'Air* similarly disabled. However, the Luftwaffe was not quite as proficient as expected. During the afternoon of 10 May, German machines ordered to strike an airfield at Dijon mistakenly dropped their bomb loads on Freiburg in south-west Germany, 140 miles away, killing or wounding 150.

While Fedor von Bock's infantry-heavy Army Group B, consisting of twenty-nine divisions (including three of panzers), made a great show of grinding its way through the Netherlands and Belgium towards the French frontier, Gerd von Rundstedt's Army Group A, consisting of forty-five divisions, containing most of the Wehrmacht's armour (seven panzer and three motorised infantry divisions), quickly sliced its way through the lightly defended Ardennes, and into open country beyond. The military theorist Basil Liddell Hart once called the German manoeuvre a 'matador's cloak', since Allied attention was drawn to the Wehrmacht's advance in Flanders, while the real *Schwerpunkt* ('main point') emerged from the woods of the Ardennes to the south.

Not realising there was any threat from the Ardennes, the majority of the BEF, with the better French forces, hotfooted it into Belgium in search of a meeting engagement with Army Group B. An additional complication was Belgian neutrality, which had prevented either ally from surveying the terrain or rehearsing tactics prior to the German invasion. There were shades of 1914–18 all over again, as a second generation of khaki-clad Tommies, clutching the same Lee–Enfield rifles, wearing the same distinctive headgear as their predecessors, flowed into Flanders. Yet, soon, under air and ground attack, the British fell back in good order, but still unaware until too late of the Rundstedt Army Group's activities to their rear.

Having crossed the Meuse and with no fixed defences or formations to oppose them, Rundstedt's armoured units fanned out, causing fear and panic. By 21 May, 2nd Panzer Division had reached the Channel coast after eleven days of combat, cutting the Anglo-Franco-Belgian defending forces in two. It was an amazing feat of arms, aided by millions of French refugees taking to the roads to flee before a second generation of field-grey-clad invaders. Ignoring the entreaties of local officials to stay put, these civilians clogged the main arterial routes used by the Allies as they tried to move forward, and died like flies in their flight, felled by fear, exhaustion, and lack of food and water, as well as by marauding German aircraft. Estimated at between 6 and 10 *million*, this great movement of Gallic peoples is still referred to in French history books as *l'Exode* (the Exodus). Behind the tanks laboured German infantry divisions, reliant more on ponies than panzers, who were twice counter-attacked by Colonel de Gaulle's tanks, on 17 and 19 May. At Arras on the twenty-first, a scratch force of British armour and infantry hit and temporarily surprised Erwin Rommel's 7th Panzer Division, causing his armour to pause awhile.

With the BEF and other allies trapped between Army Group A, to their south and west, and Bock's Army Group B to their east, and in danger of being captured or destroyed, the local British commander Lord Gort, with Churchill's agreement, ordered his forces to withdraw to the Channel ports early on 23 May, ready to take ship for England. Thereafter the British front fell back towards the Channel coast, like a slowly deflating balloon. Boulogne fell on 25 May and Calais the next day. Churchill despaired of saving the BEF, shoehorned into the small port of Dunkirk, and entirely reliant on their maritime chums to pluck them to safety.

At the same hour, George VI led a 'National Day of Prayer' in Westminster Abbey, the first time the population was made aware of the potential catastrophe facing them and their army. Events had fast degenerated from Chamberlain's announcement of war, made on another Sunday eight months before. France, the world's superpower of its time, and in praise of whose military Churchill had earlier exclaimed, 'Thank God for the French army!' – for it far outnumbered the Germans in tanks, field guns and men, if not in the air – was on its knees.

In 1939–40, Churchill attended nine meetings of the Anglo-French Supreme War Council (SWC) as First Lord; he attended five more in France during May–June 1940 as Prime Minister. On his sixth day as premier, having received a desperate phone call from his French opposite number, Paul Reynaud – in which Reynaud announced: 'We are defeated; we have lost the battle' – Winston, though in considerable danger, made the first of three flights to Paris for emergency meetings of the SWC, where he was told France no longer possessed a strategic reserve. On 26 May according to Churchill's memoirs, his sixteenth day in office, Reynaud 'dwelt not obscurely upon the possible French withdrawal from the war', revealing the aged Marshal Pétain, hero of Verdun, was already pressing for an armistice to alleviate the plight of the millions of refugees.

Presciently, in 1932 Winston had observed: 'France, though armed to the teeth, is pacifist to the core,' and thus

felt obliged to shore up the disintegration of French governmental morale he was witnessing before his eyes. Meanwhile,
with Churchill, Chamberlain, Attlee and Eden in attendance,
on 28 May Halifax urged the acceptance of an offer from
Mussolini for a general peace conference, which underlined
the continued presence in government of appeasers. Winston
put the suggestion to the full Cabinet of twenty-five members,
telling them:

> I have thought carefully in these last few days whether it
> was part of my duty to consider entering into negotiations
> with *That Man* [Hitler]... The Germans would demand
> our fleet – that would be called 'disarmament' – our naval
> bases, and much else. We should become a slave state...
> I am convinced every man of you would rise up and
> tear me down from my place if I were for one moment
> to contemplate parley or surrender. If this long island
> story of ours is to end at last, let it end only when each
> one of us lies choking in his own blood upon the ground.

As he later remembered it: 'Quite a number seemed to jump
up from the table and come running to my chair, shouting
and patting me on the back.' The Labour MP and Minister
of Economic Warfare (who would establish the Special
Operations Executive) Hugh Dalton, recorded in his diary
'a great deal of cheering', and there was no more discussion
of negotiation or surrender.

As the French government evacuated southwards, aircraft bearing Churchill with fighter escorts pursued them
on ever-riskier journeys, first to Briare, eighty miles south of

Paris, on 11–12 June, where he first met and was impressed by de Gaulle, and later to Tours, on 13 June, on the eve of French capitulation. Churchill tried a last desperate gamble to shore up French morale on 16 June, speaking to Reynaud by phone and proposing an 'Anglo-French Union, with joint citizenship, foreign trade, currency, war cabinet and military command'. Approved by Churchill's war cabinet, it meant France and Great Britain would be a single nation, in which 'every citizen of France will enjoy immediately citizenship of Great Britain, every British subject will become a citizen of France'. It came too late, with defeatists suggesting this was a plan to steal French colonies, and Pétain arguing it would amount to 'fusion with a corpse', meaning Britain. Reynaud resigned and was replaced by the eighty-four-year-old Pétain, who immediately asked for an armistice with Germany.

The extended-citizenship idea was an extreme example of Churchill fully embracing the concept of coalition warfare, which bore fruit with the later establishment of the Supreme Headquarters Allied Expeditionary Force (SHAEF), under the US general Dwight D. Eisenhower, before D-Day. More immediately, it would be a collaboration of allies in the forthcoming Battle of Britain – when Polish, Czech, Free French, Belgian, American and Irish pilots came together with their British and Commonwealth air-force brethren – who confronted and beat the Luftwaffe.

At sea and on land, these and other national contingents, including Danes, Dutchmen, Luxembourgers, Norwegians, Greeks, Palestinians, Spaniards, even some Jewish Austrians and Germans, and later Italians, would make significant coalition contributions when British and empire reserves of manpower were at their lowest. By contrast, Hitler never understood the notion of a coalition partner as an equal. Foreign detachments and governments who assisted Berlin in any capacity from 1940 to 1945 were rarely respected, often given inferior equipment and commonly blamed for any setbacks which arose.

The day after Calais fell, the cross-Channel evacuation, Operation Dynamo, began from Dunkirk, estimated to rescue 30,000 troops, with the twenty-first day of Churchill's premiership, 31 May, marking the height of the escape. On 28 May, Belgium unilaterally surrendered. With each day the military situation seemed to worsen. It is almost impossible to conceive the adversity of Churchill's position, never mind the personal stress the sixty-five-year-old would have been under so soon into his administration.

The movement of shipping and personnel to and from Dunkirk was initiated and sustained from scratch by Bertram Ramsay (1883–1945), a retired admiral recalled to the colours to oversee the Dover Straits. This again illustrated the Churchillian network in action. Ramsay's father, Colonel William, had been one of Winston's commanding officers in India. The future admiral used to spend long summers with his father, and got to know the latter's most junior officer, Churchill. We now know the younger Ramsay was among those who brought classified files about the paucity of naval spending for Churchill to study during his Wilderness Years. The pair were old friends, trusting each other implicitly, and Winston needed to say very little to his admiral to convey the gravity of the situation, or tell him what to do. In an era before specialised landing craft, to rescue the Allied armies

Ramsay assembled 900 vessels, around half of which were sunk or damaged, including six British and three French destroyers lost, nineteen more damaged, more than 200 British, French, Belgian and Dutch craft such as trawlers, ferries, lifeboats and pleasure boats from Britain's inland waterways (the famous 'little ships') wrecked – plus 145 RAF aircraft shot down.

By 4 June, Ramsay's brilliantly executed 'miracle of deliverance' (as Churchill described it), which saw 338,226 British, French and Belgian troops rescued from Dunkirk, was over. Operation Dynamo brought the admiral a well-deserved knighthood from his relieved and grateful monarch. Central to the legend of British pluck in the face of adversity, it soon became the subject of an emotional novella (Paul Gallico's *The Snow Goose* of 1941), and has since been the subject of numerous non-fiction accounts and documentaries, three stirring motion pictures, of 1958, 1964 and 2017, and, based on Ian McEwan's novel, a moving scene in the film *Atonement* (2007).

Often forgotten, another 140,000 Britons were pushed westwards, to be rescued between 15 and 25 June from France's Atlantic ports, notably Nantes and Saint-Nazaire. Sailing from the latter, the commandeered liner *Lancastria*, packed with around 6,000, received four bombs from marauding German aircraft. She went down, taking more than 3,500 with her, easily Britain's worst ever maritime disaster, and one Churchill ordered hushed up for morale purposes. He conducted as transparent a war as he dared, but, in the darkest moments, resorted to 'D-notice' news blackouts.

Aware much of the Third Reich's official news was but a distant cousin to truth, the government rarely used censorship in wartime Britain, preferring its citizens to self-regulate their speech, prompted by highly successful 'Careless Talk Costs Lives' posters. However, on 24 November 1941 Churchill would again feel obliged to invoke a reporting ban. This time it was for the sudden loss of the battleship *Barham*, torpedoed by a roving U-boat off the Egyptian coast with the loss of 862 crew. She capsized and blew up in less than five minutes, a drama caught by a Pathé news cameraman. The Admiralty only announced the loss two months later.

Winston instructed the media to present Dunkirk as a victory, but was privately nervous about having repeated the centuries-old formula of Britain's army retreating to the bosom of the Royal Navy, established at Corunna in 1809 and repeated at Gallipoli in 1916. It was still too soon to understand that May 1940 amounted to a Franco-Belgian collapse, rather than the successful application of German military doctrine. That the Wehrmacht was unstoppable seemed axiomatic, but that the Nazi machine had suffered great losses of aircraft, men and equipment, was crucially reliant on horses not panzers, possessed a minuscule war fleet – even smaller after the Norwegian campaign – had no amphibious capability at all, and was being micromanaged (far more than the British forces were by Churchill) by their ignorant Führer, was not generally understood. In short, it was in no state to invade. At this moment, Churchill again addressed the Commons, for they and the nation expected the Germans to follow up their runaway victory in France with an immediate assault on Britain. He needed to unite the country as never before.

The famous speech of 4 June was the moment at which the Prime Minister unleashed the full force of his oratory on the Commons.

> We shall fight in France, we shall fight on the seas and oceans, we shall fight with growing confidence and growing strength in the air, we shall defend our island, whatever the cost may be. We shall fight on the beaches, we shall fight on the landing grounds, we shall fight in the fields and in the streets, we shall fight in the hills; we shall never surrender.

The alliterative and repetitive effect was electric, both to seasoned MPs used to great oratory and to listeners at home, who later heard extracts read by a BBC newscaster. MP Harold Nicolson, Parliamentary Secretary at the Ministry of Information, thought the peroration 'the finest speech I ever heard'. His wife, Vita Sackville-West, responded: 'It sent shivers down my spine.' The historian Andrew Roberts reminds us: 'Churchill managed to combine the most magnificent use of English: usually short words, Anglo-Saxon words, Shakespearean.' He contends Churchill also had 'this incredibly powerful delivery. And he did it at a time when the world was in such peril from Nazism that every word mattered.'

Immediately, Chips Channon MP, a noted Churchill critic, observed: 'He was eloquent and oratorical, and used magnificent English; several members cried,' while Labour member

Josiah Wedgwood observed: 'That was worth a thousand guns and the speeches of a thousand years.' The occasion was one of the few memories of the war years my father, then seventeen, vouchsafed to me when discussing his early life. The full text still crackles with electricity and always will. As a twenty-three-year-old officer in India, Churchill had written an essay called 'The Scaffolding of Rhetoric'. In it, the future premier observed: 'The climax of oratory is reached by a rapid succession of waves of sound and vivid pictures.' Which is what his key wartime speeches achieved. Even today they have the power to move, and are a very personal extension of Churchill's unique approach to power.

With Eden's LDV up and running – unlike in France, Belgium or the Netherlands, where there were no armed citizen militias to slow down or halt German advances – Churchill started forming other ad hoc military units. Only recently have the activities of his most secretive of secret organisations, the 'Auxiliary Units', authorised on 17 June, been pieced together by author and researcher Andy Chatterton. These were teams of civilian volunteers – colloquially known as 'scallywags' – instructed to disrupt a German occupation with acts of sabotage and assassination, deploying from Hobbit-like underground 'operational bases', some of which remain remarkably intact, equipped with wirelesses, food, weapons, ammunition and chemical toilets. Scallywags' service was expected to be brief and dangerous, with a projected life expectancy of twelve days. Suicide was expected if capture beckoned.

It soon became apparent Churchill was a great advocate of special-purpose troops, sometimes known disparagingly as 'Winston's warriors', or as his 'private armies'. On 6 June 1940 Winston authorised the scallywags' uniformed equivalents, the first army Commandos. These were far more numerous, multiskilled raiding parties designed to hit Axis troops in carefully planned behind-the-lines operations. They were in business as early as 24 June, with Operation Collar landing in France, in the words of novelist Evelyn Waugh, who was one, to 'biff the Hun'. Their name was inspired by the Boer commandos, whom Churchill had fought, and been captured by, forty years earlier. Later, nine Royal Marine battalions were reorganised as Commandos, joining their army brethren in combined Commando brigades. By 1942, the Commando idea had spread to the US Army, who created their direct equivalents, Ranger battalions, equipped by America, but trained by the British.

On 22 June 1940, Churchill authorised the establishment of Britain's sky warriors, the Parachute Regiment, a counterpart to the German *Fallschirmjäger* who had spearheaded attacks in Belgium and the Netherlands. A significant force multiplier, they would eventually form seventeen battalions, but at the time were criticised, as were the Commandos, for removing much skilled manpower from ordinary infantry battalions. On 22 July, Churchill would go on to demand the creation of 'scallywags abroad', the Special Operations Executive (SOE). They were tasked with, in Churchill's phraseology, 'setting Europe ablaze' by assisting local underground movements in acts of destruction and intelligence-gathering against their German occupiers. SOE would be copied by the Americans and named the Office of Strategic Services (OSS), the first US overseas spy agency, which in 1947 became the CIA.

On 18 June Churchill again strode into the Commons for what was to prove his third key wartime address. He was responding to Marshal Pétain's earlier request for an armistice with Hitler, and might have paused to consider that the day marked the 125th anniversary of Waterloo. After a remarkably candid assessment of the battle just fought in France, and of Britain's losses and ability to carry on the fight, he intoned:

> What General Weygand called the 'Battle of France' is over. I expect that the battle of Britain is about to begin. Upon this battle depends the survival of Christian civilisation. Upon it depends our own British life, and the long continuity of our institutions and our Empire. The whole fury and might of the enemy must very soon be turned on us.

He concluded with a call to arms: 'Let us therefore brace ourselves to our duties, and so bear ourselves that if the British Empire and its Commonwealth last for a thousand years, men will still say, "This was their finest hour."' Here again, Churchill's messaging was directed far beyond British shores, at the empire and the United States, to whom he had made references earlier in the speech. This was the exclusively Churchillian concept of English-speaking peoples uniting as one against the Nazi menace.

A second speech was made on this day, overlooked in the English-speaking world, but of vital interest to the French. Charles de Gaulle (1890–1970), Undersecretary of State for National Defence and War since 5 June, had twice flown to meetings in London – on 9 and 16 June – to coordinate strategy, reciprocating Churchill's visits. After the second gathering, France's youngest general returned home to find he was no longer a minister and in danger of arrest. The next day, he had escaped back to London with no possessions, no legitimacy, few prospects, but extraordinary self-belief. On the following day, over the BBC's airwaves, and repeated on 22 June, he implored his fellow countrymen not to be demoralised, and to resist the German occupation. 'Honour, common sense and the interests of the country require that all free Frenchmen, wherever they be, should continue the fight as best they may... I, Général de Gaulle, am undertaking this national task here in England.'

He concluded:

> I call upon all French servicemen of the land, sea, and air forces; I call upon French engineers and skilled arma-ments workers who are on British soil, or have the means of getting here, to come and join me... I call upon all Frenchmen who want to remain free to listen to my voice and follow me.

It remains a red-letter day for France, and was the beginning of an extraordinary friendship and rivalry between two sim-ilarly minded alpha males. Churchill and de Gaulle helped each other in their hours of need, yet clashed repeatedly, as the former had done with Fisher and would later do with Brooke. Their alliance was vital to both nations, and no British Prime Minister has ever been so patriotic – or so Francophile.

CHAPTER 8

Finest Hour

W HAT was the cost of all this stress to Winston? The formidable Clemmie certainly noticed a growing abruptness in her husband's dealings with the Prime Ministerial staff, and on 27 June penned Churchill an extraordinary letter, of which this is an extract:

> My Darling Winston – I must confess that I have noticed a deterioration in your manner; and you are not so kind as you used to be.
>
> It is for you to give the orders and if they are bungled – except for the King, the Archbishop of Canterbury and the Speaker, you can sack anyone and everyone. Therefore, with this terrific power you must combine urbanity, kindness and if possible Olympic calm. You used to quote: 'On ne règne sur les âmes que par le calme' [souls can only be ruled by calm]. I cannot bear that those who serve the Country and yourself should not love, as well as admire and respect you.

Besides you won't get the best results by irascibility and rudeness. They will breed either dislike or a slave mentality (rebellion in wartime being out of the question!)
Please forgive your loving devoted and watchful

Clemmie

I wrote this at Chequers last Sunday, tore it up, but here it is now.

Chastened, there was a marked improvement thereafter in Churchill's behaviour to those around him, a tribute both to Clemmie's forthrightness and to Winston's ability to accept criticism without rancour.

Within a week, Churchill's levels of stress soared dramatically when he was forced to attack his former ally, France. Following the 22 June armistice with Hitler, Pétain's Vichy regime assumed its declaration of neutrality was sufficient to reassure London the French war fleet would not be handed over to the Nazi Reich. While some vessels sailed to British control at Plymouth, Portsmouth and Alexandria, the main fleet – at anchor in Mers-el-Kébir, near Oran, on the coast of French Algeria – warned it would resist any approach. Winston and the war cabinet judged the risk too great of Europe's second-largest force of capital ships reflagging to the Kriegsmarine (the German war navy). With great reluctance, Churchill ordered Operation Catapult, to neutralise or destroy the remaining warships.

In what Winston termed 'the most hateful decision, the most unnatural and painful in which I have ever been concerned', he directed Admiral James Somerville's Mediterranean Fleet to open fire on 3 July. They killed 1,300 Frenchmen, allies until a fortnight earlier, and sunk or damaged three out of four battle-ships. The act was a huge propaganda coup for Germany, while de Gaulle, who had been recognised as leader of the Free French Forces only days before, on 28 June, was furious. However, Roosevelt, who recognised the necessity for ruthlessness, let it be known he would have done the same. Churchill, who had offered the French nation dual citizenship only weeks before, remained deeply troubled by the decision for the rest of the war. It was an act for which a minority of Frenchmen never forgave him. However, it was only after this move that the Conservative benches unanimously gave him a rousing cheer for the first time, bringing political safety and relief; up until then some had remained sceptical and resolute Chamberlain–Halifax loyalists.

Meanwhile, the army had returned from Dunkirk, and was busy rearming, reorganising and commandeering civilian vehicles, having left every tank, artillery piece and truck, plus many rifles and machine guns, behind in France. The LDV had been mobilised (Churchill having personally directed their uninspiring title to be changed to the 'Home Guard' on 22 June, effective the following month), and with the Auxiliary Units recruited, what of the German threat to storm the Kent and Sussex shingle and overcome the seafront novelty-rock emporium in Bognor Regis? Churchill's daughter-in-law Pamela recalled a dimly lit dinner in Downing Street at which Winston discussed the prospect of invasion. He proclaimed: 'You can always take one with you.' Pamela, nonplussed at the prospect of taking on a steely-eyed German stormtrooper, turned to her father-in-law. 'What can I do if they come?' With a grin, he replied: 'You, my dear, may use a carving knife.'

Sharing Winston's bulldog spirit, George VI refused MI6's plea to be evacuated to Canada and pronounced: 'My family is going to stay and fight... I want to get my German and kill at least one of the invaders; we will all fight to the last.' Whereupon the Prime Minister sent the royal family a tommy gun with the note: 'You'll need this to be able to kill more than one.' His wife and daughters Elizabeth, then fourteen, and Margaret, ten, also learned to use it. On appearing for one of his weekly audiences, it greatly enthused Churchill to discover the royal family and equerries all practising with pistols, rifles and Churchill's tommy gun in the grounds of Buckingham Palace.

The wartime relationship between the King and his first minister is consistently underestimated. It began tentatively, Churchill having backed Edward VIII in the abdication crisis, but evolved into one of close mutual regard and dependency, which continued under Elizabeth II. Under Churchill's tutelage, George VI grew into his unplanned kingship, and it is not an exaggeration to assert that, following the abdication year of 1936, which nearly destroyed the monarchy, Winston materially helped haul it back from irrelevance and possible extinction.

The initial German threat came not from sea or land, but from the air. To enable a safe passage across the Channel for a summer–autumn invasion, Grand Admiral Erich Raeder of the Kriegsmarine demanded the neutralisation of Britain's air force. Thus, the Anglo-German struggle passed to Reichsmarschall Hermann Göring's (1893–1946) air arm, the Luftwaffe. After a reconnaissance phase, for the Germans had no detailed plans, the two great aerial armadas began to clash on a daily basis in late June, with their battles reaching a peak in mid-September.

Churchill knew the head of Fighter Command, Air Chief Marshal Sir Hugh Dowding (1882–1970), had created an integrated air-defence system at Bentley Priory earlier in the 1930s. It incorporated the volunteer Royal Observer Corps and included radar stations, which plotted the moves of hostile and friendly aircraft; anti-aircraft batteries and barrage balloons, which defended targets from the ground; and fighter aircraft, directed from control rooms. Command centres, operated nationally, regionally and locally around the clock, received data from all these assets, filtered and rebroadcast it to the regions and their organisations, and generally oversaw and coordinated battles. Enabled by wireless, telephone, plotting tables and electronic charts, it was unlike anything seen before, and the system became the forerunner of every large control room which today runs blue-light emergency services, power grids, railways and logistics fleets. Ever technically curious, on 16 August Churchill, along with General 'Pug' Ismay, visited No. 11 Group's command bunker at RAF Uxbridge, which controlled fighter interceptions for all of the south-east of England, and watched the Battle of Britain in play.

Though fully aware of the twenty-one (later far more) British radar stations, for they could hardly miss the 364-foot radar towers bristling along England's coastline, the Luftwaffe were less cognisant of the 'Dowding System' and constantly perplexed by the speed with which RAF fighters vectored onto and broke up their attacking air fleets. The RAF in turn were unaware of how many fighter aircraft and pilots the Luftwaffe had lost in the Battle of France, that each squadron was low in numbers, and its surviving pilots physically exhausted. The Reich's economy was sluggish and inclined to over-engineer: it had yet to switch to wartime measures, disperse manufacture, recruit women or streamline production, all measures already initiated in Britain. Further advantages played into British hands: limited in range by their fuel gauges, every German plane shot down over British soil was unrecoverable; soon picked over by RAF intelligence; their surviving aircrew taken prisoner, while each RAF pilot parachuting to safety was soon back in the cockpit of a replacement machine. Those landing at sea stood a good chance of being rescued by the RAF's Air Sea Rescue Service.

Churchill also ensured the new Ministry of Aircraft Production, established on 14 May 1940 under his friend Lord Beaverbrook (the former Max Aitken, an old political colleague, Privy Counsellor and newspaper magnate), dispersed its factories to many shadow sites, so a single raid could not seriously disrupt airframe assembly. Thus, when the Supermarine factory in Southampton was hit and destroyed in two daylight raids between 24 and 26 September 1940, the national output of Spitfires was not seriously upset. Under Beaverbrook, British aeroplane production was soon outstripping the Reich's, and despite losing 1,744 aircraft of all types in the Battle of Britain, the RAF would end up with more warplanes than it had started with. The Luftwaffe suffered 1,977 craft destroyed, with nearly all of their aircrew killed or captured, which Germany was far slower to replace.

Having predicted the Battle of Britain in his 'finest hour' speech of 18 June, Churchill analysed the aerial combat two months later, while the greatest of all air battles was still under way. Addressing a packed House of Commons on 21 August, he issued a rallying cry to his air warriors to raise their morale and proclaim to the country and wider world that Britain was still in business. As *Hansard* reported:

> The gratitude of every home in our island, in our Empire, and indeed throughout the world, except in the abodes of the guilty, goes out to the British airmen who, undaunted by odds, unwearied in their constant challenge and mortal danger, are turning the tide of the world war by their prowess and their devotion. Never in the field of human conflict was so much owed by so many to so few. (Prolonged cheers.)

Churchill had used the last seventeen words spontaneously when speaking to Ismay when visiting Uxbridge five days earlier. They had entered his subconscious and surfaced when most needed, and are an example of how many of his memorable phrases were recycled for appropriate moments.

Notwithstanding the defeat of the Luftwaffe's air assault throughout the summer and autumn of 1940, Londoners were subjected to bombing raids for fifty-seven nights from 7 September, in a deviation from German strategy. In November, the Blitz – *Unternehmen Seeschlange* (Operation Sea Snake) to the Germans – soon spread to the port cities of Bristol, Cardiff, Portsmouth, Plymouth, Southampton, Sunderland, Swansea, Belfast and Glasgow, as well as industrial centres like Birmingham, Coventry, Manchester and Sheffield, pausing only in February 1941. The King, Queen and the Churchills were quick to visit the bombed areas, the Prime Minister directing a message of national solidarity under German bombs be emphasised in all print, radio and newsreel media, primarily as a propaganda tool for domestic and foreign consumption. It began a tradition, continued to this day, of the nation's leaders speedily visiting sites of dramatic misfortune. It was a grim time: at the end of September Churchill learned 6,594 civilians had been killed by German bombs during that month alone, and, on 21 October, the 500th British merchant ship had been sunk. Yet, the same night, he felt able to broadcast in upbeat mood: 'We are waiting for the long-promised invasion. So are the fishes.'

In 1991, historian Angus Calder challenged the Churchillian view that the British population, divided by the class conflict and political infighting of the Depression years, overcame their internal fissures and united in defiance of daily bombing raids. In his revisionist *The Myth of the Blitz*, Calder argued interpretations of the triad of Dunkirk, the Battle of Britain and the Blitz were based on wartime propaganda, rather than historical reality. Clive Ponting's *1940: Myth and Reality* (1990) also explored this territory, with both books contending, contrary to the fallacy of what Calder called 'serene national unity', class division persisted, while looting and other crimes soared. Nevertheless, a broad cross section of society did indeed remember it as Britain's 'finest hour'.*

---

* Many of John Charmley's meticulously documented works, particularly *Chamberlain and the Lost Peace* (1989); *Churchill: The End of Glory* (1993); and *Churchill's Grand Alliance* (1995), also amount to revisionist reappraisals of the 'Finest Hour'. They contend that numerous scholars have romanticised the events of 1938–45, suggest some kind of truce with Germany was possible in 1940, and argue that Chamberlain, who 'left no stone unturned to avoid war', has been unjustly maligned by proponents of Churchill's version of history.

On 14–15 November 1940, a major raid by 515 bombers (*Unternehmen Mondscheinsonate* – Operation Moonlight Sonata) ripped out the heart of Coventry, destroying 4,300 homes and killing or injuring 1,500. Foreshadowing Bomber Command's later attacks on Germany, the raiders used pathfinder aircraft with electronic aids to navigate and mark their targets before the main force arrived with high-explosive bombs, air mines and incendiaries to set the city ablaze in a firestorm. Several post-war authors have claimed Churchill had advance warning of the raid via secret intelligence but ordered no defensive measures be taken in order to protect his sources. Archives have effectively demolished this assertion. While signals intelligence had warned Churchill a major raid would take place, no one knew where, and most assumed it would be London.

Through his speeches and visits, Churchill had braced the nation for the worst possible scenario, called everyone to arms and attracted the attention of the wider world to Britain's plight. However, only if fortune smiled and they survived would the United States climb off the fence and join them. It was not just America's might that was required, but her industry. Britain needed vast quantities of war materials which could only come from across the Atlantic. As the country's gold reserves would soon be exhausted, loans and credits would have to be negotiated, but Churchill was aware Roosevelt first needed to focus on his presidential re-election campaign.

Winston, meanwhile, remained largely absent from the airwaves over the next few months while he ranged across the United Kingdom, busy shoring up morale after visiting the sites of heavy air raids. Painfully cognisant a year of war-making had already cost Britain half its gold reserves, Churchill was gratified to hear Roosevelt was offering to provide equipment for ten British divisions, but dismayed to discover $257 million was being asked in advance. Diplomatic relations eased greatly when the pro-appeasement and defeatist US ambassador Joe Kennedy was dismissed by Roosevelt in October 1940. Unlike other diplomats stationed in the capital, he insisted on quitting London nightly during the Blitz, leading Winston's son Randolph to observe: 'I thought my daffodils were yellow until I met Joe Kennedy.' He was replaced in February 1941 by the far more likeable John G. Winant, who became a lover of Sarah Churchill and whose aviator son would be shot down over Germany and sent to Colditz.

Churchill could see America was edging closer to aiding him, if not actively entering the war, as Roosevelt's press conference of 17 December 1940 made clear:

> Suppose my neighbour's home catches fire, and I have a length of garden hose four or five hundred feet away. If he can take my garden hose and connect it up with his hydrant, I may help him to put out his fire... I don't say to him before that operation, 'Neighbour, my garden hose cost me fifteen dollars; you have to pay me fifteen dollars for it'... I don't want fifteen dollars: I want my garden hose back after the fire is over.

In January 1941, Roosevelt's special advisor, Harry Hopkins, landed in Britain, and the pair began to hammer out a solution to the 'garden hose' issue, soon known as the Lend-Lease Act, signed on 11 March 1941. The United States would build and ship what Britain needed and lease it on a rental basis, with payment delayed until after the war. In the meantime, Britain would forward as much as she could in gold. Before his return, Hopkins announced that his recommendation to Roosevelt was to offer unfaltering support, quoting the words of the biblical book of Ruth: 'Whither thou goest, I will go; and where thou lodgest, I will lodge; thy people shall be my people, and thy God, my God.' Hopkins paused, then whispered: 'Even unto the end.' Charles McMoran Wilson (later Lord Moran), Churchill's personal physician, who witnessed the scene, later remarked that, to the tearful Prime Minister, the words 'seemed like a rope thrown to a dying man'. Hopkins immediately reported back to Roosevelt that Winston was the 'directing force behind the strategy and conduct of the war in all its essentials. He has an amazing hold on the British people of all classes and groups.'

This was the context of Churchill's next major speech, on 9 February 1941, aimed unequivocally at the United States. He began with a candid survey of Britain's fortunes:

> Five months have passed since I spoke to the British nation and the Empire on the broadcast. In wartime there is a lot to be said for the motto: 'Deeds, not words.' All the same, it is a good thing to look around from time to time and take stock, and certainly our affairs have prospered in several directions during these last four or five months, far better than most of us would have ventured to hope.

He concluded memorably, addressing Roosevelt personally:

> Put your confidence in us. Give us your faith and your
> blessing, and, under Providence, all will be well. We shall
> not fail or falter; we shall not weaken or tire. Neither
> the sudden shock of battle, nor the long-drawn trials of
> vigilance and exertion will wear us down. Give us the
> tools, and we will finish the job.

At sea aboard the battleship *Barham*, Surgeon Commander
E. R. Sorley wrote home, summarising the reaction of many
to the speech:

> Thank God for Winston Churchill at this time. I think
> that was the predominant feeling amongst us at the end of
> his most moving speech. There is no other man on earth,
> I believe, who can inspire us with the spirit of dogged
> resolution and fierce desire to strike our enemies; who
> can so combine the art of moving oratory with the bite
> of ferocious justified invective.

America understood Churchill's message and, apart from the
lifeline of Lend-Lease, responded with the motion picture *Mrs
Miniver*, a romantic war drama written in 1940 about an
unassuming housewife in rural England (Greer Garson) whose
husband takes his boat to Dunkirk. Their house is bombed and
she captures a wounded German aviator in her garden. It con-
cludes with a sermon by the local priest in his bombed-out and
roofless church, delivered in unmistakably Churchillian tones:

This is not only a war of soldiers in uniform. It is the war of the people, of all the people. And it must be fought not only on the battlefield, but in the cities and in the villages, in the factories and on the farms, in the home and in the heart of every man, woman, and child who loves freedom. Well, we have buried our dead, but we shall not forget them. Instead, they will inspire us with an unbreakable determination to free ourselves, and those who come after us, from the tyranny and terror that threaten to strike us down. This is the People's War. It is our war. We are the fighters. Fight it, then! Fight it with all that is in us! And may God defend the right.

Churchill blubbed all the way through his private screening; America got the message and gave it six Oscars. Although *Mrs Miniver* reached cinemas only in 1942, when the acute crises of 1940–41 had receded, it was matched by a British film of the same year, *Went the Day Well?*, adapted from a story by Graham Greene, which portrayed an English village captured by German paratroopers, and the way its inhabitants fought back against their invaders.* A favourite of Churchill's, when he had time for private film viewings, it was an equally frank reassurance to America – plucky Britain would survive.

---

* Winston was alive to the propaganda value of patriotic films for a population who visited cinemas on a weekly basis, and encouraged productions of *That Hamilton Woman* (1941), about Nelson; *The Next of Kin* (1942), explaining the value of the 'Careless Talk Costs Lives' campaign; *Millions Like Us*, *Fires Were Started* and *The Gentle Sex* (all 1943), about war workers, the Auxiliary Fire Service and the lives of female soldiers like his daughter Mary; *The Way Ahead* (1944), the story of a group of army conscripts; or Laurence Olivier's *Henry V* (also 1944).

CHAPTER 9

Blood, Sweat and Tears

NAVAL affairs still obsessed Churchill, worried as he was by the prospect of the transatlantic supply of oil, raw materials, foodstuffs and more being severed by German submarines and surface raiders. He stated later the Battle of the Atlantic was the campaign which gave him the greatest wartime nightmares. Following extensive air raids on Plymouth, and given the city's remoteness from shipping lanes, on 7 February 1941 Churchill ordered the move of Western Approaches Command, which tracked and coordinated transatlantic convoy movements, and monitored German surface raiders and U-boats, to Derby House, Liverpool. Unbeknown to most Liverpudlians, this top-secret facility was the maritime equivalent of Dowding's integrated air-defence headquarters. Manned by 300 staff, the joint Admiralty and RAF battle centre comprised 100 rooms under a seven-foot concrete roof, housed just behind Liverpool's city hall. Huge charts of the North Atlantic and coastal waters around Britain hung in a central control room, constantly updated with information from aerial reconnaissance, convoy and warship reports and secret intelligence. It had direct lines to intelligence centres, the Cabinet and Churchill, who visited in 1941 and observed of the maritime port: 'I see the damage done by the enemy but I also see the spirit of an unconquered people.'

The value of Derby House, today open to the public, was immediately apparent when the German battleship *Bismarck* and her escorting heavy cruiser *Prinz Eugen* were spotted leaving western Baltic waters on 20 May 1941. It soon transpired they were bound for the North Atlantic to sink Allied shipping, and Winston, through his First Sea Lord, Admiral Sir Dudley Pound, directed a maximum effort to intercept them. Four days later, the battleship *Prince of Wales*, on which Churchill would soon meet Roosevelt, and battlecruiser *Hood*, the best-known warship of the Royal Navy as a result of her many world cruises, caught up with the German pair. In the Denmark Strait between Greenland and Iceland the British ships opened fire, but a shell from *Bismarck* struck *Hood* near her aft ammunition magazines. She blew up almost immediately and sank with 1,415 of her crew, leaving only three bobbing about in the freezing North Atlantic. *Prince of Wales* continued the engagement but was soon outgunned and obliged to retire.

In one of the costliest disasters to befall the fleet to that moment, the Royal Navy's flagship was gone, leaving Churchill inconsolable and demanding retribution. Much of the Home Fleet, and what could be spared from Gibraltar and the Mediterranean, were ordered to sink the offenders. Winston required hourly reports of the pursuit, which was well depicted in the 1960 film *Sink the Bismarck!* and described later in Ludovic Kennedy's book of 1974. Shadowed by cruisers and sometimes by Swordfish biplanes, attacked with torpedoes and by gunfire, *Bismarck* was eventually sent to the bottom three days later, while *Prinz Eugen* snuck back to her French Atlantic lair of Brest. The episode illustrated the rise of the aircraft carrier and demise of the battleship, for it was aircraft from *Ark Royal* which had found, shadowed and attacked *Bismarck* for much of the engagement. Had the Germans completed their own carrier, *Graf Zeppelin*, and sent her into the Atlantic with *Bismarck*, the story would likely have ended differently.

Churchill spent his premiership running Britain's war in a hands-on way beyond belief to modern politicians. He could do this partly because he left domestic policy almost entirely to Attlee, and partly because no one in the world at his level had such experience of grand strategy. When it came to Russia, Churchill found his politics at odds with his opportunism. As we have seen, he had been on his guard against the Eastern Bear ever since the time of the tsars, and was repulsed by Stalin's disregard for human life. Yet he was genuinely perplexed by the twists and turns of Soviet foreign policy.

Following his pronouncement of 1919 that 'Bolshevism is a great evil... arisen out of great social evils', he doubled down on his hostility in *The World Crisis*, likening the 1917 conveyance of Lenin across Germany to Russia in a sealed train to 'a plague bacillus and more deadly than any bomb'. Of Lenin himself, he opined: 'His weapon, logic; his mood, opportunist; his sympathies, cold and wide as the Arctic

Ocean; his hatreds, tight as the hangman's noose. His pur-
pose, to save the world; his method, to blow it up.' However,
during the interwar years his hostility to the Soviet Union
discreetly lessened as that towards Nazi Germany increased,
and, in September 1938, he had invited Russia's ambassador, Ivan Maisky (who served in London between 1932 and
1943), to Chartwell. Stalin's diplomat remembered discussing
alcohol with Churchill, who showed him the finest specimens
in his cellar, including a claret from 1793 he was 'saving for
a special occasion'. When asked what the event might be,
instantly Churchill responded, with much foresight: 'We will
drink this bottle together when Great Britain and Russia beat
Hitler's Germany!'

The social invitation, which coincided with the Munich
crisis, was much appreciated by the Russian, who was familiar with Churchill's hatred of Bolshevism and advocacy of
British military intervention in the 1919 campaign against
the Soviet Red forces. At the time of the Maisky house party,
Winston was still out of government and neither had reason
to ponder that, within twenty months, Churchill would be
Prime Minister. Nor that, in less than a year, Maisky's boss,
Molotov, would be signing a non-aggression pact with his
opposite number, Ribbentrop, in Moscow.

In its aftermath, with the division of Poland, Churchill
illustrated his understanding of the larger wheels of history
and geopolitics in an October 1939 broadcast:

> I cannot forecast to you the action of Russia. It is a riddle
> wrapped in a mystery inside an enigma. But perhaps there
> is a key. That key is Russian national interest. It cannot

be in accordance with the interest or the safety of Russia
that Germany should plant itself upon the shores of the
Black Sea, or... overrun the Balkan States and subjugate
the Slavonic peoples of south-eastern Europe. That would
be contrary to the historic life-interests of Russia.

The international picture changed when Hitler invaded the
Soviet Union on 22 June 1941, something he had long threatened, even in the pages of his polemic *Mein Kampf*, published
in 1925. The same evening Winston took to the airwaves to
build on his friendship with Maisky, offer Stalin his unequivo-
cal support and conclude: 'No one has been a more consistent
opponent of Communism than I have... I will unsay no words
that I've spoken about it. But all this fades away before the
spectacle which is now unfolding.' This was the beginning of
what Churchill termed the 'Grand Alliance', to be joined by
the United States within seven months. Writing in his diary,
Maisky, who days before had noted he was 'disinclined to
believe that Hitler will attack us', recorded Churchill's words
were suitably 'bellicose and resolute: no compromises or
agreements! War to the bitter end!'

On 8 July, Churchill messaged Moscow: 'We shall do
everything to help you that time, geography and our growing
resources will allow.' In August 1942, he flew via Egypt and
Tehran to Moscow to meet Stalin in his lair, discuss Lend-
Lease and warn the Soviet leader there would be no landings
in France (the 'second front' for which Russia was lobbying)
for at least a year. Ignored by modern Russian historians but
recorded by *Hansard,* from 1 October 1941 British ships bore
to the Soviet Union 5,218 tanks; 7,411 aircraft and 976 aero

engines; 4,020 trucks and ambulances; 2,560 Bren Carriers; and 1,721 motorcycles – while the Admiralty transferred one battleship, nine destroyers, four submarines and fourteen minesweepers, all fully provisioned with spares, ammunition, radar and wireless equipment, collectively valued at £308 million.

Later, at the behest of Clemmie, chair of the Red Cross Aid to Russia Fund, who travelled to Moscow for her own fact-finding five-week tour, another £110 million worth of clothing, blankets, X-ray machinery, medical supplies and other hospital equipment was also delivered, of which £8 million was underwritten by public subscription. This not inconsiderable effort, represented by seventy-eight Arctic convoys, would cost Churchill eighty-five merchant vessels and sixteen Royal Navy warships sunk, with most of their crews lost.

During the war, Churchill needed to escape the attentions of the Luftwaffe on London, as well as the claustrophobia of his bombproof Cabinet War Rooms, built under the Foreign Office, from where he often ran his campaigns, spoke to Roosevelt by scrambler telephone and consulted his maps. In his quest for the calm of England's rolling acres it was obvious his beloved Chartwell was too well known as his country retreat and too dangerous, being on the Luftwaffe's flight path to London, and consequently it was mothballed during 1940–45. Likewise, the official Prime Ministerial residence of Chequers, with its long, straight drive covered with pale stone, seemed to beckon to German bombers. Under a full moon, the pathway appeared to shine like an arrow pointing to the house. In *The Splendid and the Vile*, author Erik Larson discovered a reminiscence of Churchill at Chequers, clad in his blue one-piece 'siren suit' and silk dressing gown, clutching his personal Mannlicher stalking rifle, and, to the strains of martial music from a gramophone, practising bayonet drills on a 'German' cushion.

Soon, Churchill was offered a refuge at Ditchley Park, not far from Blenheim and near Oxford, which nestled inconspicuously in a park of mature trees. During his Wilderness Years, Churchill and Clemmie had been pre-war guests of its owner, the anti-appeaser MP Ronald Tree, and used it in lieu of Chequers from November 1940 to March 1943, it being large enough to accommodate Winston's by now impressive entourage plus a company of troops to guard the place. Both the Cabinet War Rooms and Ditchley are vital stops on any Churchill pilgrimage, as is the next venue.

In 1938, the secret Government Code and Cypher School had moved into an ugly mansion near Milton Keynes, acquiring the house and secluded grounds cheaply on the death of its previous owner. Bletchley Park, known as 'Station X', was soon expanded to include a collection of unlovely wooden army huts and cheap brick offices for the 9,000 scientists, cryptographers, translators, intelligence analysts and secretaries who slowly gravitated there on a task as furtive as that of the Auxiliary Units. What they did was remarkable. Having been supplied by Polish intelligence with an Enigma enciphering machine, used by most German ministries and all military detachments, from army units to Luftwaffe squadrons and submarines, they reverse-engineered the device to crack its 'unbreakable' coded transmissions, used hourly by the minions of the Reich.

The boffins succeeded in reading German confidences for much of the war; contributed to advance knowledge of the November raid against Coventry (although the target wasn't known at the time); helped defeat the *Bismarck*; were able to warn Stalin of the impending invasion of Russia (although this was ignored); fed intelligence to the naval command centre in Liverpool; and were the linchpin in winning Churchill's nightmare-inducing Battle of the Atlantic. Naval interpretations, classified as 'Ultra Secret', or 'Ultra' for short, originated from Hut 4, today's visitors' canteen, where the first Enigma codebook, snaffled from a sinking U-boat in May 1941, was used for naval codebreaking.

However, there was much dissatisfaction among staff with the primitive and crowded accommodation and lack of leisure facilities. When one staff member wrote to Churchill about their difficulties, the Prime Minister responded with a personal visit on 6 September 1941. He assured them their highly compartmentalised efforts were of a war-winning nature, allocated money for sports, recreation and better conditions, and awarded them the accolade of being 'my geese that laid the golden eggs and never cackled'. Thereafter, the car park became tennis courts, the only ones built by Prime Ministerial decree.

Yet over-reliance on Enigma decrypts or misunderstanding them brought problems. With or without his 'golden eggs', Churchill's strategy-making could be dangerously off-key. One example was the unravelling of his Mediterranean and North African strategies in 1941. Under General Archibald Wavell (1883–1950), British forces pulled off several brilliant campaigns against the Italians between June 1940 and April

1941. The most spectacular took place in the Western Desert along the Libyan–Egyptian border, where Mussolini's Tenth Army had lurched forward, crossed the Egyptian frontier, advanced sixty miles, and then stopped and dug in.

Correctly sensing his opponents' hesitancy and lack of confidence, in Operation Compass Wavell counter-attacked with his Western Desert Force (later to find fame as Montgomery's Eighth Army) in December 1940, pushing his opponents back to Tripoli and taking 130,000 prisoners ('several dozen acres of captives', as one staff officer wrote home), together with their equipment and supplies. At Mussolini's request, in February 1941 Hitler deployed a small detachment called the Afrika Korps, under the then-obscure Erwin Rommel, to rescue his embarrassing ally. And there the Enigma problem began. Station X warned Wavell of Rommel and his orders from Berlin. Yet the talented, unorthodox and highly aggressive 'Desert Fox', as he was soon known, attacked against orders, before his units were complete, and retook all of Wavell's gains, which Bletchley Park could not have anticipated.

Churchill was furious with his taciturn and distant commander, who was given to writing poetry and, in his words, 'resembled the chairman of a suburban golf club'. Yet the talented Wavell had been obliged by Winston to shift many of his best troops from Libya to Greece after the conclusion of Compass, leaving less experienced men in the desert. In 1939 London had offered Athens a security guarantee, and so when, following a lacklustre invasion from Italian-occupied Albania into Greece, Mussolini's 1940–41 march faltered, RAF squadrons were soon operating against them from

Greek airfields, while Wavell was told to send a corps-size force comprising Britons, Australians and New Zealanders to Piraeus harbour. Like the debacle in North Africa, this brought the Germans galloping to the rescue of their Fascist friends. A swift Nazi blitzkrieg struck northern Greece, pushing the Allies back, and, with the loss of three fully loaded troopships and two destroyers, the Royal Navy rescued the remnants of the 50,000-strong force over 24 April–1 May, leaving behind a number of personnel, vehicles and masses of equipment.

'Wars are not won by evacuations,' growled a humiliated Churchill, yet for the second time his navy had plucked his army from the jaws of certain disaster. Wavell's Greek force, under the adopted New Zealander Bernard Freyberg (1889–1963), was now evacuated to Crete. Freyberg, holder of a Victoria Cross and three Distinguished Service Orders, was one of Winston's favourite generals, whom he nicknamed 'the Salamander' (for his supposed ability to withstand all wounds and fire). He was another of Churchill's old network who, in 1914, had been commissioned into the Royal Naval Division after an interview with its founder, Winston. In the 1930s 'the Salamander' was a not infrequent presence at Chartwell dinner parties, where the host delighted in insisting the impossibly bemedalled Freyberg remove his dinner shirt so guests could count his twenty-seven wounds. The modest warrior always retorted only half 'were proper injuries caused by bullet or splinter, the rest being exit wounds left by the departing steel and lead'. Churchill took instantly to Freyberg, a true, *Boy's Own*, larger-than-life character, and remained under his spell.

On Crete Freyberg's men were threatened with an Italo-German assault from sea and air. Forewarned by Station X of the new Axis plan and their order of battle, Freyberg judged the seaborne threat to be the most potent and deployed his men along Crete's northern coastline. In fact, the Royal Navy managed to sink the approaching seaborne invaders almost to a man, but it was the legions of German *Fallschirmjäger* (paratroops) and glider-borne infantry dropping from the clouds on 20 May who proved his undoing. Freyberg's poorly resourced and tired defenders, arrayed mainly to oppose an amphibious landing, were slow to wake up to the extinction of the maritime threat and the imminent arrival of an airborne one. (Post-war, Freyberg would mischievously claim he dared not risk realignment to receive paratroops and gliders in case of compromising the top-secret intelligence flow from Station X.)

Supported by endless streams of Stuka dive-bombers which seemed to attack the slightest shadow, Germany's sky soldiers soon took the three major airfields on Crete, whose significance Freyberg's staff had failed to recognise, and, sustaining their invasion solely by air, swiftly overran the island. Freyberg's force was fast elbowed to the south of Crete, and, in Britain's third maritime evacuation in a year (the fourth since Norway), was pulled from the tiny port of Sfakiá between 28 May and 1 June. Some 12,000 were left behind and taken prisoner. Much blame could (and probably should) have been directed at Freyberg for his handling of Crete, but his friendship with Winston ensured 'the Salamander' shook off any opprobrium and was soon in action again.

'I have been in a serious battle and have decided I abominate military life. It was tedious and futile and fatiguing. I found I was not at all frightened; only very bored and very weary,' wrote the waspish novelist Evelyn Waugh of his experiences on Crete with a Commando outfit known as 'Layforce'. He would go on to pen *Officers and Gentlemen* (1955), whose central chapters deliver the author's real-life experiences of the battle, via his fictional proxy Guy Crouchback. Waugh was evacuated by destroyer, one of many the Mediterranean Fleet deployed to rescue the army and its allies, but at huge cost.

Hostile aircraft and surface vessels sank four Royal Navy cruisers and six destroyers, including Lord Louis Mountbatten's *Kelly* on 23 May, an event which inspired Noël Coward's patriotic war film of 1942, *In Which We Serve*. Faced with such drastic losses, the Admiralty ordered the evacuation to cease, but the local naval commander, Admiral Andrew Cunningham, retorted: 'It takes the Navy three years to build a new ship. It will take 300 years to build a new tradition,' and continued. Also damaged were the carrier *Formidable*, battleships *Warspite* and *Barham*, four cruisers, two more destroyers and a submarine, putting them out of action for months.

While the destruction of *Bismarck* on 27 May distracted British public opinion, Churchill was incandescent at the loss of Greece, Crete and the warships, as well as the setbacks in North Africa, and blamed Wavell. In fact, they were the result of misunderstanding Enigma decrypts, but principally caused by Churchill's own interference. His general could have triumphed over the Italians and Rommel had he been allowed to keep his Western Desert Force intact in Egypt, but the warlord insisted the much-maligned Wavell divide his legions, with the result both halves were beaten. With so many ships lost or damaged, Churchill was warned the Mediterranean Fleet 'had been pushed to breaking point'.

An army officer evacuated from Crete remembered sailing into Alexandria, where:

> every warship was down at the bows or stern, or listing this way and that; their hulls and funnels were plastered with dents and holes from shrapnel splinters, decks strewn with ammunition, their bleary-eyed crews struggling to make them serviceable again. One cruiser, the *Penelope*, was so riddled that we christened her 'Pepperpot'.

More directly, Crete led to the establishment of another of Churchill's private armies, still in business today. As Freyberg's force had failed adequately to defend Crete's aerodromes, Winston decreed the air force assume responsibility with the formation of the RAF Regiment, effective from 1 February 1942. Henceforth, air-force personnel trained as infantry would be responsible for protecting aerodromes on land and providing local air defence. Churchill ensured they had an offensive role, too, in seizing and securing enemy airfields, intelligently enmeshing land-based operations with air power.

On 4 August, Churchill set sail aboard the repaired *Prince of Wales* for his first journey outside Britain since the fall of France, bound for a maritime rendezvous with Roosevelt. 'It is 27 years ago today that the Huns began their last war. We must make a good job of it this time,' he cabled the American President. An account of the voyage was penned by the popular travel writer H. V. Morton, chosen to accompany Churchill's entourage, which appeared as *Atlantic Meeting* in early 1943. Arriving in Placentia Bay off Newfoundland five days later, the 'Big Two' began the first of their thirteen wartime meetings, which concluded on 12 August with a mutual-aid agreement known as the Atlantic Charter. Both leaders saw this, their first summit, as a turning point in the unfolding conflict. It reaffirmed America's desire to help Britain, but not yet to enter the war.

CHAPTER 10

Unrelenting Struggle

A NOTHER Churchillian misjudgement emerged in the wake of the Japanese assault on the US Pacific Fleet at Pearl Harbor during the Sunday morning of 7 December 1941. The following day Congress declared war on Tokyo, and Roosevelt telegraphed Churchill using an unfortunate metaphor: 'Today, all of us are in the same boat... and it is a ship which will not and cannot be sunk.' Back in October, Churchill had proposed dispatching a force of three capital ships to protect Malaya and Singapore in the event of Japanese aggression in the Far East. Named 'Force Z', originally it was slated to comprise the battleship *Prince of Wales*, battlecruiser *Repulse*, carrier *Indomitable* and four escorting destroyers. In November *Indomitable* ran aground en route, necessitating twelve days of dry-dock repairs. Nevertheless, Churchill, with his exaggerated belief in the power of the battleship, intervened to insist Force Z deploy, publicly announced its departure on 1 December, 'to deter the Japanese', and directed that air cover in the form of *Indomitable* or another carrier would follow later.

On 8 December Force Z left Singapore to intercept a Japanese invasion fleet reported in the South China Sea, north of Malaya. They were spotted by Japanese aircraft and submarines, followed and attacked on 10 December. From 11 a.m. *Prince of Wales* and *Repulse* were bombarded by waves of torpedo-carrying aircraft, though the commanding admiral initially elected to maintain radio silence. A request for aerial assistance was not sent until an hour into the Japanese assault. There were other problems, including extreme heat and humidity, which rendered *Prince of Wales*'s anti-aircraft fire-control radars unserviceable and affected some of her ammunition. Ignoring the destroyers, the marauding aircraft concentrated on the two capital vessels, and, for the loss of three planes, scored four torpedo hits on each. *Repulse* succumbed first, rolling over at 12.33. The more modern *Prince of Wales* lasted until 13.18 before the waves closed over her hull. Ironically, land-based air cover assigned to protect Force Z appeared over the battle area at the very minute *Prince of Wales* disappeared. It would have arrived earlier, and possibly saved them, had the ships asked for aerial help sooner.

The vessels should never have deployed without a carrier, and were the first to be sunk solely by air power while steaming in open sea. With two major warships down and 840 sailors dead, and following the raid on Pearl Harbor, the Allied capital fleet in the Pacific was reduced to just three US carriers and no large battleships at all, which prompted Churchill finally to realise the potency of naval air power, and the susceptibility of warships to it. These losses triggered a huge dent in morale across the region, severely weakened the British Eastern Fleet in Singapore, and were instrumental in the 15 February 1942 surrender of the colony to Japan. Despite Churchill's experience of naval matters, his knowledge was already out of date, and the ships' demise was another example of the warlord's sometimes destructive interference.

However, Churchill was not one to brood on disaster, and, on Saturday, 13 December, two days after Hitler's bizarre declaration of war on America, Winston boarded the battleship *Duke of York*, sister to the *Prince of Wales*, braving gale-force winds, and arrived at Norfolk Navy Yard, Virginia, on the twenty-second. He would not return to London until 17 January 1942. Winston could now breathe a sigh of relief that the United States was irrevocably committed to joining him in the global struggle. It was the realisation of all his strategic hopes since May 1940. As he hurried to confer with Roosevelt and expand the growing 'special relationship', staying at 1600 Pennsylvania Avenue, Washington DC, burned 127 years earlier by other Britons, and better known as the White House, he knew Britain and her empire were no longer alone, and his darkest nightmares were over.

This was the first of the 113 days the two leaders would spend together, with Churchill staying at the White House on four different occasions. At the series of conferences he and his military staff held with their opposite numbers in Washington (collectively code-named 'Arcadia'), it was agreed to invade French North Africa in the autumn of 1942 (Operation Torch) and northern France in 1943; here too was established the Combined Chiefs of Staff Committee (unifying the British and American chiefs), whose secretary was to be the industrious Brigadier Dwight D. Eisenhower.

Putting Churchill up in the Rose Room, White House staff soon found they had to adapt to Winston's working routines. Another chamber was converted into a map room, while his entourage carried on with their day-to-day business of taking dictation and scurrying around with correspondence, reports and speeches. The late-night dinners followed, and the morning routines of baths, newspapers and more correspondence. The Chinese-silk bathrobe was there, though the assorted tumble of pets had stayed in England. Roosevelt's staff later recalled this first visit left the impression of a renewed British occupation, with Churchill usurping the President's role of running the war. This was the time when the wheelchair-bound Roosevelt arrived at his guest's bedroom and caught Winston emerging, in the words of Harry Hopkins, 'stark naked and gleaming pink from his bath'. As Roosevelt apologised and made to withdraw, Churchill protested: 'The Prime Minister of Great Britain has nothing to hide from the President of the United States.' As he later reported to George VI: 'Sir, I believe I am the only man in the world who has received the head of a nation without any clothes on!'

Swiftly, the two agreed to call the coalition fighting the Germans, Italians and Japanese the 'United Nations'. On the twenty-third they held a joint press conference; on Christmas Day they attended morning church, and, on 26 December, Churchill addressed a joint meeting of Congress, the first of three occasions when he spoke to both houses. He opened with a winning reference to his Brooklyn-born mother, Jennie: 'I cannot help reflecting that if my father had been American and my mother British, instead of the other way round, I might have got here on my own. In that case, this would not have been the first time you would have heard my voice.' The appreciative laughter and applause continued for minutes and partly explains Churchill's continuing popularity on both sides of the Atlantic. The same evening, he experienced what he called 'a dull pain over my heart'. His personal doctor, Wilson, suggested slowing down, but Churchill continued with his packed programme and headed to Ottawa.

The Canadian capital proved memorable for two reasons. To its parliament he delivered a twenty-two-page, thirty-seven-minute speech, constantly interrupted by cheers and applause. Its highlight came when Winston cited his last communiqué to Pétain's collaborationist government in June 1940. 'When I warned them that Britain would fight on alone whatever they did, their generals told their Prime Minister and his divided Cabinet, "In three weeks England will have her neck wrung like a chicken."' Churchill paused for a moment: 'Some chicken!' Another pause. 'Some neck!'

It brought the house down.

After a drink in the speaker's chambers, Churchill agreed to pose for a portrait by the talented but then little-known Ottawa photographer Yousuf Karsh. In jovial mood, Churchill bounded into the room, whisky in hand, puffing at a cigar. Karsh, who thought there were already too many photos of Churchill with a cigar, approached the Bulldog and whipped it out of his mouth. 'By the time I got back to my camera,' Karsh recollected afterwards, 'Churchill looked so belligerent he could have devoured me.' The scowling image of his subject elevated Karsh to world fame and remains the most remembered picture of the wartime leader. The Canadian premier, Mackenzie King, was delighted and sent three copies to Churchill with the note: 'I think you will agree the photograph is one of the best, if not the very best, ever taken of yourself.'

Meanwhile, matters seemed to have gone from bad to worse in North Africa: Churchill was perplexed none of his generals seemed to be able to outfox the Desert Fox, Rommel. Safely returning to Blighty by flying boat, in the House of Commons on 27 January 1942 Winston felt moved and chivalrous enough to say of his adversary: 'We have a very daring and skilful opponent against us, and, may I say across the havoc of war, a great general.' His comments went down poorly at home, and with the Eighth Army, and two days later Winston was at the receiving end of a motion of 'no confidence in the central direction of the war'. This was the penalty for micromanaging British strategy. So closely associated was he with its direction that when excessive setbacks occurred, Westminster, the press and the country turned on him. The debate took place on 29 January 1942, in the wake of the Mediterranean and Far Eastern reverses.

Another such motion would be debated on 2 July, again largely the result of his 'daring and skilful opponent' continuing to run rings around the Allied forces (which now included Australian, British, Free French, Greek, Indian, New Zealander, Polish and South African detachments) in the Libyan desert. Although only one member voted against Churchill in the January motion, and twenty-five in July, it underlined the transparency of British democracy in action: general elections, held theoretically a maximum of five years apart, had been suspended since September 1939, though parliamentary business continued. Despite Churchill's personal discomfort, such a procedure was in pleasing contrast to the dictatorships of Italy, Germany and Russia. Winston himself had used the device of a motion on 13 May 1940 to reaffirm the formation of his coalition government, when it was carried unanimously, but the later instances illustrated his vulnerability, for, in the event of losing a confidence motion, Westminster tradition obliged the government to resign, or seek a dissolution and call a general election. The 1940 Norway debate had concluded with such a motion against Chamberlain, which, although won by 281 to 200, still caused his resignation as Prime Minister two days later.

Although there were moments when Churchill faced the music alone, such as the 1940 speeches (where he presented excessively rehearsed monologues, patiently redrafted according to the great man's whim by squadrons of secretaries always in attendance and to whom he dictated throughout his working day, from his first morning bath to the small hours), the Prime Minister's style tended towards delegation, tempered by constant interference. Faced with irregular hours, where weekends ceased to exist and Prime Ministerial tantrums were common, his personal staff did not rebel as Clemmie feared they might. One spoke for many when he described proximity to Churchill as 'the feeling of being recharged by contact with a source of living power'.

The Prime Minister forged a war-winning relationship with Field Marshal Sir Alan Brooke (1883–1963), his French- and

German-speaking and long-suffering Chief of the Imperial General Staff, a role he occupied from 1941 to 1946, who calmed the Prime Minister's wilder ideas and enacted the sanest. Possessed of equally strong personalities, the pair represented the most effective team of any nation's political–military leadership during the Second World War. Like Clemmie, Brooke saw his role as standing up to Churchill, recording the latter as 'genius mixed with an astonishing lack of vision – he is quite the most difficult man to work with... but I should not have missed the chance of working with him for anything on earth', whereas Churchill noted of 'Brookie': 'When I thump the table and push my face towards him what does he do? Thumps the table harder and glares back at me.'

With the 2 July 1942 confidence motion still ringing in his ears, in August Churchill and Brooke flew separately to Cairo to assess the situation in North Africa, where Wavell's successor, Sir Claude Auchinleck (1884–1981), commander-in-chief of the British forces in the Middle East and running the Eighth Army, was having difficulty in besting his opponent, Rommel. Although receiving strategic intelligence from Station X at Bletchley, 'the Auk' was not to know the Germans were reading the correspondence of the American defence attaché in Cairo, revealing all his plans, and also had a very good front-line signals-interception company in action, providing real-time battlefield intelligence. Perceiving command problems at the highest level in Egypt, Churchill flew out via Gibraltar, arriving in the desert heat on 4 August, where he stayed at the British embassy in Cairo.

He was depressed by the briefing he received from the talented but shy and awkward Auchinleck at his 'unimpressive and flyblown headquarters' in the desert. By contrast, the RAF's pipe-smoking, genial Air Chief Marshal Arthur Tedder (1890–1967) provided a very upbeat assessment of the campaign of his Desert Air Force, 'supplemented by food hampers from Cairo's premier kitchen, Shepheard's Hotel'. On 6 August, Churchill consulted the former Boer commando turned leader of South Africa, Field Marshal Jan Smuts (1870–1950), whose counsel he greatly valued, before flying on to Moscow via Tehran on the ninth. En route, he decided to relieve the Auk. He pondered possible replacements while away for his first meeting with Stalin. Surviving the Russian leader's wrath that any date for a second front had now slid into 1943, and a series of excessive drinking sessions known to the Soviets as diplomacy, Churchill returned to Cairo on 17 August, conferred with Brooke and decided on the Auk's replacements.

The new men were to be Sir Harold Alexander (1891–1969) as theatre commander, with General William Gott (1897–1942) under him leading the Eighth Army. However, spies in Cairo had alerted the Germans to Churchill's presence, and the Luftwaffe targeted his plane for what we now know to have been a mid-air assassination attempt. It was shot down, but the unlucky man aboard was not Winston but Gott, travelling from the front to Cairo to meet his new staff. Churchill and Brooke had to think again. Brooke suggested Bernard Montgomery (1887–1976), well known as a ferocious trainer of men, but who had last seen combat in May 1940.

Though neither recalled their first meeting at the Lille victory parade in 1918, Churchill had come across 'Monty' when inspecting the coastal defences of south-east England in the summer of 1940. Shocked one of his generals refused wine over dinner, the Prime Minister heard the teetotal Montgomery explain he 'neither drank nor smoked and was 100 per cent fit'. Churchill immediately responded: 'I both drink and smoke and am 200 per cent fit,' thus beginning another competitive friendship between two strong characters. In the event, Monty's health, though impaired by bullet damage to his lungs in 1914, would prove more robust than Winston's. Thus it was that the relatively unknown Lieutenant General Montgomery was summoned from England and thereafter led the Eighth Army with great panache to win the Battle of El Alamein that autumn (23 October–11 November), subsequently taking them into Tunisia, Sicily and southern Italy.

At the end of a packed programme of meetings in Cairo and Moscow, replete with gastronomic and alcoholic excess, and interspersed with several long-distance flights in unpressurised aircraft, each at risk of aerial interception, Winston returned to England to be greeted by Clemmie after an absence of twenty-three days. It would have been a challenging schedule for a man of half his sixty-seven years.

CHAPTER 11

Onwards to Victory

E LSEWHERE, between May and November 1943 a killer famine arose in the Indian province of Bengal (now divided between modern-day Bangladesh and the Indian state of West Bengal), which has since been interpreted by some historians as having been caused or exacerbated by Churchill. As one of the favourite tropes continually deployed against the reputation of the wartime leader by anti-colonialists and Indian nationalists, it is important to examine it closely. The facts are these. The famine is beyond question, and a six-month period of hunger took place when the Japanese were occupying neighbouring Burma, had invaded north-east India and bombed Calcutta. Estimates of the death toll range between 1 and 3 million.

The case for the prosecution is built partly on Churchill's hostility to Indian independence during the 1930s and his alleged prejudices against non-white peoples. Yet his antipathy was more a reflection of his strategic concern for India to remain a pro-British bulwark against possible Russian expansion, or any other rival power, than personal animosity. Though Winston had a blind spot about Mahatma Gandhi, it didn't necessarily extend to the wider Indian population, of whom over 2.5 million had volunteered to serve in the British cause by 1945. In July 1944, Churchill was heard by Alan 'Tommy' Lascelles, the King's private secretary, to say the outdated view of the inferiority of the Indian should be abolished: 'We must all be pals together,' the Prime Minister added – hardly the sentiments of a Churchill wishing to commit genocide by starving the Indian people, as the American Bengali author Madhusree Mukerjee alleges. There was much goodwill and interaction between Britons and Indians: this author's father was stationed in India for some of his war and, when not training his Royal Artillery detachment, played in the Calcutta Symphony Orchestra, welcomed as the only European in a sea of Indian faces.

When food shortages began to arise, they had nothing to do with Churchill, being, according to the historian and broadcaster Zareer Masani, 'largely the result of wartime supply constraints, with most of Bengal's boats commandeered or disabled, and uneasy relations between the elected, Muslim-led, coalition government of Bengal and its largely Hindu grain merchants, notorious for hoarding and speculation'. Churchill initially regarded the situation as the responsibility of the viceroy's government in Delhi and the regional authorities in Bengal, rather than Whitehall. His Cabinet in London, busy fighting a world war, assessed their role as one of broad oversight rather than detailed management. However, India Office archives reveal that, when they were made aware of the acute problem, over a million tons of Iraqi barley and Australian wheat were dispatched, despite Japanese submarines skulking in the Bay of Bengal, to be distributed by British military logistics, thus destroying claims of food aid deliberately withheld.

On 24 September 1943, Churchill stated in Cabinet 'something must be done', and on 7 October, he announced the viceroy was to see 'the famine and food difficulties were dealt with'. He decreed: 'Every effort must be made, even by the diversion of shipping urgently needed for war purposes, to deal with local shortages.' Subsequently, on 14 February 1944, Churchill wondered if even more could be sent without hindering plans for the impending D-Day invasion, though he later admitted: 'We have given a great deal of thought to your difficulties, but we simply cannot find the shipping,' a view echoed in Washington, assessing they needed all their merchant vessels for the Pacific theatre and the upcoming Normandy invasion, but by then the crisis was over. However, Bengal was not alone, for Kenya, Tanganyika and Somaliland also suffered famine at the same moment, and, as Masani observes, summarising the conclusions of Andrew Roberts's biography: 'Far from seeking to starve India, Churchill and his Cabinet sought every possible way to alleviate the suffering without undermining the war effort.'

In other areas, Winston's vision of the Allied war effort clashed with that of the Americans. The US Army chief of staff, George C. Marshall (1880–1959), was ready to invade France in 1942, and had to be dissuaded by Churchill and overruled by Roosevelt from committing such an error, for his army was not remotely combat-ready, as setbacks at Kasserine Pass (18–24 February 1943), after the mostly unopposed Torch landings, proved. By the time the Italo-German force in North Africa had surrendered at Tunis on 13 May 1943 (an event labelled 'Tunisgrad' by Churchill as his version of the Red Army's earlier victory at Stalingrad), it was again too late to contemplate invading France.

Thus, Washington acquiesced in Winston's proposed strategy of immediately invading Sicily (Operation Husky, fought from 9 July to 17 August 1943), where Admiral Ramsay, victor of Dunkirk, deposited slightly more US, British and Canadian troops than he would in Normandy on 6 June 1944, and spread over more beaches. Amphibious landings on the southern Italian coast followed in September, but drew the Americans further away from their goal of a Normandy invasion. Twice, it seemed to the Americans, Churchill had managed to talk them out of invading northern France, and some privately wondered if he had cold feet on account of overseeing the Gallipoli assault in 1915.

However, in conferences at Casablanca over 14–23 January 1943 (collectively code-named 'Symbol'), Churchill agreed to the establishment of an Anglo-American tri-service headquarters to plan for future landings in France, which were disguised by the code name 'Overlord', the first use of the now-famous moniker. This was also the moment at which, at Marrakech, he executed his only oil painting of the war, with which we started this volume. Over 12–15 May, Churchill again conferred with Roosevelt and Marshall in Washington DC (code name 'Trident'), taking the opportunity to address a joint session of Congress for a second time and thrashing out more of the minutiae for Overlord. Later that year, at the Tehran Conference of 28 November–1 December

1943, the first wartime meeting of the 'Big Three' (code-named 'Eureka'), Eisenhower was chosen to command the Normandy invasion.

There is evidence Churchill offered to exchange American control of Overlord for British dominance in the Mediterranean, where Sir Harold Alexander was proving a popular coalition commander. Besides, having Overlord run by an American was a good insurance policy should anything go wrong, as Winston feared possible. However, both Churchill and Brooke hoped the attritional slogging match of the Western European war would be decided in the boxing ring of the Mediterranean under British leadership, even if Overlord were to deliver the final knockout blow. Both Churchill's *Second World War* and Brooke's diaries reveal the pair as passionate supporters of their Mediterranean-first policy, which would have seen Italy conquered and subsequently the Balkans or south of France invaded in 1944. However, the strategic truth was, with the Americans now fielding the lion's share of manpower and equipment, they would be taking the most casualties, and not unreasonably should dominate Allied strategy. An insight into Churchill's anxieties over D-Day came on the eve of invasion, when he dined alone with Clemmie and confided: 'Do you realise that by the time you wake up in the morning 20,000 men may have been killed?' His fears were unfounded, with the total proving to be under 25 per cent of his nightmare, but, twenty-nine years on, he remained haunted by the failure of Gallipoli.

Thus, the cards lay on the table indicating Normandy, and an operation led by the American Eisenhower, to whom the

British airman Arthur Tedder had been appointed deputy, enabled by a fleet again assembled by Bertram Ramsay, and set for May–June 1944. The day itself proved to be Britain's supreme contribution to the defeat of Germany, for 80 per cent of Ramsay's supporting warships, around 60 per cent of the air force and over half the troops involved on the day of assault itself, twice delayed to Tuesday, 6 June, were British or Canadian. Churchill was determined to be there and had secretly arranged to take passage with the invasion fleet aboard the cruiser *Belfast*. It was during their lunchtime audience of 30 May 1944 that Churchill mentioned it to the King, for technically a Prime Minister cannot travel abroad without the monarch's consent. George VI was not only enthusiastic, but felt he should be there too, at the head of his navy.

It was only when Lascelles, his private secretary, and Queen Elizabeth issued all sorts of warnings of constitutional crises should the pair perish that His Majesty was dissuaded, but not his Prime Minister. Poor Admiral Ramsay was caught in the middle, concerned Winston was 'only there for a joy ride'. Eisenhower got to hear, and as overall commander vetoed the scheme, but the sixty-nine-year-old Winston petulantly replied he would make himself a bona fide member of *Belfast*'s crew. Administered by the Imperial War Museum, the 11,550-ton town-class cruiser is today moored in the Thames. We now know Churchill would have been perfectly safe aboard her, but how poignant it would have been for a brass plaque to be set into her deck, reading: 'Here stood Winston Churchill on 6 June 1944'. However, it was not to be. Eventually the King pleaded with his Prime Minister not to go, and Churchill grudgingly assented.

Other Churchills were heavily involved in the assault wave, however. British and Canadian engineer regiments, equipped with Churchill tanks, named in the Prime Minister's honour, attacked German bunkers, or, with flamethrowers or temporary combat bridging, forced their way through Rommel's beachfront obstacles. Winston and George VI soon visited the front, Churchill on D+6 (12 June), the King four days later. From Portsmouth, Churchill was conveyed to the invasion front by the destroyer *Kelvin*, going at thirty knots. Normandy hove to in only four hours. As the BBC reported:

> A naval salute was given to Mr Churchill's arrival on shore: three salvoes on the German lines. Soldiers busy unloading landing craft stood in amazement at the sight of the familiar Trinity House cap, cigar and two fingers raised in a V-sign. Some stood to attention and saluted, others held back, waved, clapped and cheered.

He was particularly keen to see the artificial harbour in operation at Arromanches, christened 'Port Winston', for he had been involved in its design. Churchill had long foreseen the need for some kind of floating harbour to sustain a seaborne invasion and directed research into Meccano-like components, writing to Lord Louis Mountbatten: 'They must float up and down with the tide. The anchor problem must be mastered... Don't argue the matter. The difficulties will argue for themselves.' The date, 30 May 1942, was a full two years before he inspected the finished product.

Winston picnicked with Monty at his headquarters, punctuated by the crump of large naval shells whistling overhead. The mess waiter produced Camembert cheese, not seen in England since 1940. Of the bucolic scene, Churchill observed to Brooke the 'fat cattle lying in luscious pastures with their paws crossed', and later recollected, with a hint of disappointment:

> The General [Monty] was in the highest spirits. I asked him how far away was the actual front. He said about three miles. I asked him if he had a continuous line. He said 'No'. 'What is there then to prevent an incursion of German armour breaking up our luncheon?' Monty said he did not think they would come.

The Prime Ministerial presence, so soon after D-Day itself, proved a huge tonic to all who saw him. 'I had a jolly day on Monday on the beaches and inland... How I wish you were here!' he cabled to Roosevelt on his return.

After a grinding six-week campaign in Normandy, with an average daily attrition rate which exceeded the Somme or Verdun in 1916 and Third Ypres in 1917, the Western Allies eventually broke through the region's signature hedgerows, the *bocage*, encircled the Germans at Falaise in mid-August, then raced for the German border. Montgomery, now commanding the Anglo-Canadian army group, resisted Churchill's attempts to get him to deviate and overrun the V-1 launch sites, whose flying bombs had started to plague London from 13 June. Later the general clashed with his American colleagues and his boss, Eisenhower, on several occasions, but was protected by Brooke and Churchill, for Monty was their creature, on whom they had risked their reputations back in August 1942.

Yet Montgomery was prickly and arrogant: to many he lacked diplomacy and tact. Paradoxically, his directness made him a good military leader and popular among his men. But not necessarily Churchill, who was known to quip: 'In defeat, unbeatable; in victory, unbearable.' After El Alamein, when told Monty had given dinner to the first German general captured, Ritter von Thoma, Winston immediately remarked: 'Poor von Thoma; I, too, have dined with Montgomery.'

Having spent 10–29 August in Italy, in the aftermath of the Monte Cassino campaign and liberation of Rome, and witnessed the French Riviera landings on the fifteenth, Winston paraded down the Champs-Élysées with de Gaulle on 1944's Armistice Day, and with victory peeping over the horizon, one might have expected Churchill to enjoy a relaxed Christmas somewhere in England. But no. In Greece, the influence of the Communist Party within the resistance movement he had backed throughout the war – the National Liberation Front – had grown stronger than expected, and seemed likely to jeopardise Winston's plan to return the Greek king to power and keep Communism at bay. Before the war, Greece was ruled by a royalist dictatorship whose emblem of a fascist axe and crown well expressed its ambiguity. Its leader, General Ioannis Metaxas, had trained as an army officer in Wilhelmine Germany, while the Greek king, George II, an uncle of Prince Philip, future husband of Elizabeth II, was pro-British. Pursuing his blind faith in monarchies, Winston drove to Chequers on 23 December, where his family had already gathered for Christmas, to tell Clemmie he would be flying to Athens to sort out a civil war which had erupted in the Greek capital.

She was devastated, fled to her room and wept. Early on Christmas morning Churchill was airborne, taking Eden with him. Stopping at Naples to refuel, they reached Athens at two on Christmas afternoon. Basing himself on the cruiser *Ajax* with Communist shells falling in the sea all around them, he summoned both sides to negotiate at the British embassy. His secretary, John Colville, noted: 'While the Prime Minister was speaking, the sound of gunfire went on ceaselessly without, and at one moment the roar of descending rockets, launched by Beaufighters at some nearby enemy position, almost drowned his words.' Churchill tried to get the two sides to reconcile until 28 December, then left by armoured car for the nearest airbase, to the sound of bullets ricocheting all about, flew home, and reached a worried Clemmie the following afternoon. Within a couple of hours, he and Eden were giving an account of their hair-raising Christmas in Athens to the war cabinet, for whom the business of wartime governance knew no holidays.

Winston's Greek intervention stemmed from a boozy dinner he had shared with Stalin in Moscow on 9 October 1944. Churchill wanted to affirm the post-war 'proportional interest' of the West and Russia in five European countries, and on a handy piece of paper suggested 90 per cent Russian interest, 10 per cent Western for Romania; Yugoslavia and Hungary were listed as fifty–fifty; Bulgaria was to be 75 per cent Russian, 25 per cent Western; while Greece was listed as 90 per cent British, in order to keep Stalin out of the Mediterranean. Churchill recalled the Russian leader 'took his blue pencil and made a large tick upon it'. On 14 October, Stalin agreed fifty–fifty for Poland, but these percentages soon proved meaningless, and all would soon fall under Stalin's sway, save Greece. Yet the notional exercise had proved swifter and less painful than the redrawing of the European map in the protracted peace conferences of 1919–21 – unless, of course, you happened to be an inhabitant of one of those nations Churchill had just sold into Soviet slavery.

While Winston was dodging bullets in Athens, the US Army had been busy repelling a surprise German assault in the Ardennes (the same region where they had struck lucky in 1940). In its aftermath, on 7 January 1945, Montgomery held a press conference and claimed he had saved the day. America's generals were apoplectic. In response to Monty's comments, Churchill gave him a rare public tongue-lashing in the Commons on 18 January: 'Care must be taken in telling our proud tale not to claim for the British Army an undue share of what is undoubtedly the greatest American battle of the war, and will, I believe, be regarded as an ever-famous American victory.'

Between 13 and 15 February the Western Allies struck at Dresden, a masterpiece of baroque and rococo architecture on the River Elbe, and capital of Saxony. Some 772 British bombers, plus 527 from the US Army Air Forces, pounded the city with high-explosive and incendiary bombs, utterly destroying its historic centre and creating a firestorm which killed around 25,000. Several revisionist historians claimed Churchill ordered its destruction in retaliation for the bombing of Coventry, or fudged the true death toll.

Encouraged by Lindemann, the RAF's strategic bombing offensive had the multiple aims of weakening the morale of the German people through the destruction of their homes while hindering transportation, arms and oil production, with day-to-day authorisation of targets the responsibility of Sir Arthur Harris (1892–1984), chief of Bomber Command. However, Winston – who had been an advocate of strategic bombing ever since it was first devised as a war-winning strategy bv Marshal of the RAF Sir Hugh Trenchard in 1918 – had already started to draw back from the policy, exclaiming on 27 June 1943: 'Are we beasts? Are we taking this too far?' on watching film footage of an RAF raid on the industrial centre of Wuppertal. By 1945, there were few unmolested targets which justified a major aerial attack. However, Dresden stood out as an important armaments centre and transportation hub, through which passed road and railway traffic destined for the Eastern Front.

When the Soviet High Command requested a raid on the city to aid their advance, Harris agreed, but Churchill wasn't even in the country, instead conferring with Stalin at Yalta. In the aftermath Winston realised a new threshold of horror had been crossed, and on 28 March minuted: 'It seems to me the moment has come when the question of bombing of German cities simply for the sake of increasing the terror... should be reviewed. The destruction of Dresden remains a serious query against the conduct of Allied bombing.' Thus, the city had not been a British target for vengeance, but a Soviet one, attacked at their request for tactical military needs.

The last significant battle of the Western theatre was to cross the River Rhine in the spring of 1945, something Eisenhower always thought would be as bloody as D-Day. This time Churchill was present to watch 'Montgomery's show' on 24 March. The next day he insisted on clambering across the twisted ironwork of a bombed bridge to the German side. First, he symbolically urinated into the great river, then photographs were taken of his party before they were bracketed by German shells plunging into the river; next, hearing sniper fire, the local commander insisted they depart. 'The look on Winston's face,' wrote Brooke,

> was just like that of a small boy being called away from his sandcastles on the beach by his nurse! He put both his arms round one of the twisted girders of the bridge, and looked over his shoulder... with angry eyes!... It was a sad wrench for him, he was enjoying himself immensely.

Having achieved his main aim of coming under hostile fire for the final time, in his seventieth year, a feat first achieved on his twenty-first birthday in 1895, he flew back to London. It was a fitting 'last hurrah' for Winston the warrior.

CHAPTER 12

Liberation

C HURCHILL, Roosevelt and Stalin met again at Yalta, former summer resort of the tsars in the Crimea. The British delegation was housed in the nineteenth-century mansion of a courtier in the Scottish baronial style, with the main sessions held in the Livadia Palace, once the summer retreat of Nicholas II and his family, then a Soviet sanatorium, and latterly a German headquarters. Once 'disinfected of its Teuton occupiers', fine furniture and choice food was flown down from the best Moscow hotels. Churchill once asserted: 'Never be late for dinner, smoke a Hawaiian cigar, or drink Armenian brandy,' but at Yalta he was for once obliged to forgo his preferred French cognac and swallow an Armenian *digestif*. During more ridiculous drinking sessions dressed up as Soviet diplomacy, over 4–11 February 1945 plans were discussed for post-war Yugoslavia; occupation zones to be administered by US, British, French and Soviet forces; the provision of minimal subsistence to the former Reich; the dismantlement of all

German military industry; and an international court to try major war criminals.

Churchill claimed in his report to a boisterous and uneasy House of Commons on 27 February: 'The sovereign independence of Poland is to be maintained,' but in the same breath announced: 'I decline absolutely to embark here on a discussion about Russian good faith.' He already knew of the disappearances of Polish officers at Katyn, privately surmising Stalin's culpability, and was fully aware of the probable fate of Eastern Europe under Soviet domination. As early as the following month he concluded the Soviets were already disrespecting the 'spirit of Yalta', but realised he could do little to alter the course of events. He knew none of Western Europe, least of all a bankrupt Britain, was in any condition to fight Russia for Poland. Nevertheless, Winston directed Brooke to draw up a contingency plan to fight the USSR in 1945, which envisaged forty-seven British and American divisions, plus ten of Poles and remobilised *Germans*, attacking the middle of Soviet lines in the area of Dresden. Brooke assessed the notion as 'hazardous', with any chance of success as 'fanciful' and christened the scheme 'Operation Unthinkable'.

Yalta was the last time Churchill would see Roosevelt, the former noting he felt the latter's 'compact with life was very slim'. On 12 April 1945 his great wartime partner, friend and associate since 1918 died unexpectedly of a cerebral haemorrhage, aged sixty-three. A fellow MP noted the news came to Winston as 'a real body blow'. Churchill immediately made plans to fly out for his funeral and confer with his successor, Harry S. Truman, who was anxious to meet. A plane was readied, but then, at the last minute, inexplicably, Winston changed his mind.

None of the archives presents a convincing case as to why Churchill failed to pay his final respects in person to his great wartime ally, with whom he exchanged more than 1,700 letters and telegrams, on average nearly one a day. Perhaps he was still annoyed with FDR for often siding with Stalin at Yalta; perhaps he was tired. Perhaps he was still recovering from the death of his close friend David Lloyd George on 26 March, or perhaps he couldn't accept Britain's decline and American ascendancy in global affairs. In a 13 April letter to King George VI, he absurdly suggested: 'I think it would be a good thing if President Truman should come over here.' Although referring to Roosevelt as 'the greatest American friend we have ever known, and the greatest champion of freedom who has ever brought help and comfort from the new world to the old', when leading the mourning in St Paul's on 17 April, Winston must have realised establishing a close bond with the new man in the White House would be vital to Britain's standing in the post-war world. But it was a move he failed to make, and is one of the unexplained mysteries of his life.

On 15 April, Montgomery's forces liberated Belsen concentration camp, and Eisenhower invited Churchill to send a deputation of MPs and peers to inspect it and Buchenwald, freed by the Americans. They departed immediately, a distressed Winston telegraphing Clemmie, who was busy with her Red Cross appeal touring Russia: 'Intense horror has been caused by the revelations of German brutalities in the concentration camps.' An American newspaper editor accompanying the British and US delegations announced: 'I came here in a suspicious frame of mind, feeling that I would find many of the terrible reports that have been printed in the United States before I left were exaggerations, and largely propaganda. They have been understatements.'

Churchill's role in British domestic policy was remote and an example of his inclination to delegate, indicating that social issues did not excite him as much as strategy-making. One issue his government arguably mismanaged related to the 150,000 black American troops stationed in England before D-Day. The US Army wanted to segregate them, as in the United States, and, rather than stand up for the African American GIs, Herbert Morrison, the Home Secretary, and James Grigg, Secretary of State for War, rolled over and allowed US military policeman to enforce the separation policy in British shops and pubs, later to be termed the 'marriage of prejudice and expediency'. It proved hugely divisive, with much of the population welcoming the strange faces into their homes. It was a shameful episode, but Winston's eyes were exclusively focused on the forthcoming Normandy landings.

As much of the wartime coalition government's effort was directed to winning the war, its legislative achievement was unimpressive compared to many administrations. The exception was the 1944 Education Act, the work of R. A. Butler (1902–82), a noted pre-war appeaser of whom Churchill remained suspicious. Yet, recognising Rab's formidable intellect, and true to his inability to bear a grudge, Churchill moved Butler from a junior role in the Foreign Office to his first Cabinet position as Education Secretary. His 1944

Act raised the school leaving age to fifteen, made religious instruction compulsory and introduced selection between grammar schools and state-run secondary moderns, at the age of eleven.

Throughout the war the political parties maintained an effective consensus on almost every policy. This proved the wisdom of the Churchillian, all-inclusive, collegiate method of government. It was best expressed by the publication in November 1942 of the Beveridge Report, enabled by a cross-party, multi-departmental initiative fostered by Labour's Arthur Greenwood, a member of the war cabinet. Its author, William Beveridge (1879–1963), was an Oxford academic and former civil servant, another of Churchill's great network who worked under Winston in 1908 when the latter was at the Board of Trade.

Entitled 'Social Insurance and Allied Services', it would become, and remains, the defining tenet of the modern welfare state, advocating free healthcare, compulsory insurance and unemployment benefits for all. Although a traditionally obtuse policy paper and priced at two shillings, by 1945 it had sold 600,000 copies. Labour wished to implement the Beveridge Report forthwith, leading to a Commons debate in March 1943, but Churchill – partly on grounds of cost, as the state coffers were already empty from prosecuting the war – dictated its adoption would be post-conflict. Although a logical extension of the pre-1914 Liberal reforms with which Churchill had been associated, the Prime Minister's plan would have been a means-tested, diluted form of Beveridge. A sense of the Conservatives opposing Beveridge (who became a Liberal MP in 1944), or that they were not as committed as Labour, would contribute to Churchill's surprise electoral defeat in July 1945.

By the end of the war, Churchill had travelled hundreds of thousands of miles in unpressurised aircraft and across U-boat-infested oceans in pursuit of victory. Arguably, he was at his best when travelling, coalition-building and communicating, skills he exploited at the expense of actually governing, which he left to his deputy, Attlee. Working an average of ninety hours a week, smoking heavily, he succeeded in besting three bouts of life-threatening pneumonia (in February and December 1943 and September 1944) and a heart attack (while staying at the White House in December 1941), any of which might have felled a younger man.

Through all his medical setbacks, he continued directing the country from his bed, treating his medical and clerical staff 'as intimate friends', members of his extended family. Thus, Churchill and the nation took it for granted he would win the 1945 general election. After the defeat of Germany, 8 May 1945 was designated Victory in Europe (VE) Day and the Prime Minister appeared first on the Ministry of Health balcony in Whitehall and later on that of Buckingham Palace with the King and Queen, waving to the hundreds of thousands cheering him in exaltation and relief. If May 1940 was the nation's 'finest hour', May 1945 was Churchill's. The message he broadcast that day was already one of spinning history as he wanted to see it, but also mindful of the general election he knew to be on the horizon:

> My dear friends, this is your hour. This is not victory of
> a party or of any class. It's a victory of the great British

nation as a whole. We were the first, in this ancient island, to draw the sword against tyranny. After a while we were left all alone against the most tremendous military power that has been seen. We were all alone for a whole year. There we stood, alone. Did anyone want to give in? Were we downhearted? The lights went out and the bombs came down. But every man, woman and child in the country had no thought of quitting... Now we have emerged from one deadly struggle... Tomorrow our great Russian allies will also be celebrating victory and after that we must begin the task of rebuilding our hearth and homes, doing our utmost to make this country a land in which all have a chance, in which all have a duty.

Although he wanted the wartime coalition to continue until Japan had been vanquished, the Labour Party pressed for a dissolution, responding to its own grass roots. Attlee also pointed out there had been no general election since 14 November 1935 – nearly a decade before – which was hardly a good advertisement for British liberal democracy.

The domestic popularity of Churchill and that of the Conservatives turned out to be two separate things. The former was undimmed, but Britain remembered the mass unemployment of the interwar years, associating it with the predominantly Tory administrations of the period, and from 1942 Labour had won a string of by-elections. The Beveridge Report and Butler Education Act excited a desire for change, for a new world. The general election of 5–26 July 1945 was a uniquely prolonged business, extended because of a three-week gap in which to count the ballot papers of British service personnel scattered around the globe.

Initially, both sides found it difficult to break away from the warm consensus of the wartime coalition, which Churchill himself destroyed in an ill-judged speech of 4 June. This time his rhetoric worked against him when he claimed 'some form of Gestapo, no doubt very humanely directed in the first instance' would result from a Labour victory. His former loyal foot soldiers, Attlee, Bevin, Greenwood, Morrison and others were aghast and the electorate incredulous. The Labour victory, announced on 26 July in the middle of the Potsdam Conference, was as much a surprise as its majority of 145 seats. Even Churchill's 20,000 majority in Epping fell by 3,000 votes.

Australian historian Robin Prior assesses that both world wars were won for Britain by the imposition of political control over its military, who rarely demonstrated the strategic nous required to win. He argues Lloyd George interfered too little in 1917 and let the Passchendaele campaign run its disastrous course, though the Welshman deviously transferred blame to Haig in his own misleading *War Memoirs*. Not until the nine meetings of the Supreme War Council, established on 7 November 1917 to coordinate Allied military activity, and especially after 26 March 1918, when Foch became the Allied military generalissimo, did political control return.

By contrast, in 1940–45 Churchill interfered far too much, perhaps in subconscious compensation. The papers of his principal military advisor, Brooke, so well edited by Alex Danchev and Daniel Todman, reveal just how much he held his Prime Minister in check during those vital years.

Prior emphasises Churchill's diminishing influence, as that of America increased, which was reflected in the strategic choices the Western Allies made from 1942. Winston's obsessions with Balkan adventures and unease over landings in France were more confidently rebutted by Roosevelt and Brooke's counterpart Marshall the stronger US forces became.

In the long history of British Prime Ministers, the nation had never experienced a premier quite like him, with such a forceful personality, unique in so many ways. Not only had Churchill proved an able administrator and effective leader, but he possessed an extraordinarily curious mind. He was what we would call today an instinctive horizon-scanner and had a knack of anticipating the course of events. He wrote and speculated about future technology, surrounded himself with scientists and experts of every conceivable discipline, and developed networks of people on whom he could call for advice – a methodology which also helped when writing his major historical works. He understood and appreciated the human resources at his disposal, and although Andrew Roberts reminds us Churchill's policy was for scientists 'to be on tap, not on top', Winston trusted and listened to those inside and outside of government.

His tendency was to delegate, but with endless interference. He drove his civil servants and private appointees mad with distraction, working long hours, sparing neither himself nor those around him, but led a team who delivered victory. His endless committees had to deal with specific problems at high speed, and respond to Prime Ministerial directives when the lighthouse beam of Churchill's attention fell on their activities. During his premiership he devised a bright-red,

'Action this Day' sticker to be attached to documents requiring immediate attention, reinforcing his dictum, on entering Downing Street: 'I like things to happen, and if they don't, I make them happen.'

CHAPTER 13

Sinews of Peace

INSTEAD of leaving politics and accepting the dukedom (of Dover) offered him by King George VI in 1945, Churchill remained an MP but travelled widely to receive honours from the free world, write, paint and relax in sunnier climes. By then, the Pol Roger champagne house had reserved Winston's favourite vintage of 1928 for his exclusive use. When this ran out, what was left of 1933 was similarly put aside. Having taken up owning racehorses, Churchill returned the favour by naming one of his steeds Pol Roger, which strode to victory at Kempton Park in 1953, the coronation year. 'So many bottles, so little time,' he mused. 'I could not live without champagne. In victory I deserve it. In defeat I need it.' Pol Roger would later estimate his purchases of their reviving drink at 42,000 bottles during his lifetime.

The world showered him with gifts, including his lion Rota, leopard Sheba and two white kangaroos, Digger and Matilda. These four went to reside at London Zoo, where they proved especially popular, their keepers bidden to provide Winston with detailed progress reports. This was a time when Britons christened their male heirs 'Winston', just as others had chosen 'Nelson' in centuries past, in the hope some of the past owner's luck and magic would attend the new bearer. So did writers, including Eric Blair. Writing as George Orwell, his seminal *Nineteen Eighty-Four* (1949) featured as its protagonist the down-at-heel everyman, Winston Smith, who grappled with the nature of truth and how it could be subverted in authoritarian states of the kind seen in Berlin and Moscow.

With many wealthy friends and influential advisors in attendance, the international Churchill travelling caravan, rarely less than twenty with family and staff, acted as an informal opposition government throughout Attlee's premiership. These were golden years, when few airlines, hotels, restaurants or shipping companies felt they could charge the saviour of the free world for their services – indeed, they positively queued up to have him on their premises, gratis. For those keen on a Churchill pilgrimage, there are still many hotels and restaurants, particularly around the fringes of the Mediterranean, which boast proudly of having hosted the great man.

Being out of office acted in Churchill's favour, as it had done in the Wilderness Years. It enabled the literary factory at Chartwell to generate even greater numbers of books (ten volumes of non-fiction and ten tomes of speeches between 1948 and 1958), which served to keep his name in the public eye. Principal among these were the delightful *Painting as a Pastime* (1948), based on articles written for the *Strand Magazine* in 1921–22), and the six volumes of his *Second World War* (1948–53). He used two German prisoners of war to help clear the ground around his lakes, emptied because they might have identified Chartwell to the Luftwaffe, so they could be restocked with fish. When Churchill – naturally supervising this muddy task in person – complained it was going too slowly, he was amused to receive his own famous words by way of rebuke: 'Give us the tools and we will finish the job.' However, in maintaining both a London residence, at 27–28 Hyde Park Gate, SW7, and Chartwell, Winston was soon forced to accept the latter house and its grounds were proving too expensive to run. Then a group of generous friends, led by William Berry, 1st Viscount Camrose, and owner of the *Morning Post* and *Daily Telegraph*, struck a unique deal with the National Trust.

They raised £55,000, enabling the Trust to buy Chartwell from Churchill; in exchange for a rent of £350 per annum, Winston and Clemmie agreed to a fifty-year lease, allowing them to live there until their deaths, at which point the property reverted to the Trust, in whose hands it is now preserved. To Camrose, Winston penned his appreciation: 'I feel how inadequate my thanks have been, my dear Bill, who... never wavered in your friendship during all these long and tumultuous years.' For his eighty-eighth birthday Winston was given a marmalade-coloured cat, Jock, by his long-serving secretary Sir John Colville. Jock soon gained the status of 'most favoured pet', and when Winston died and Chartwell reverted to the National Trust, the deeds included the instruction: 'a marmalade cat with white bib and socks called Jock' should always live there. On my last visit I was able to pay obeisance to Jock VII, who I can report has acquired some of the great man's gravitas.

Out of office, Churchill was able to make speeches which as Prime Minister he might have been dissuaded from delivering. Foremost among them was the 5 March 1946 address at Westminster College in Fulton, Missouri, President Truman's home state, where he described the state of affairs in Communist Eastern Europe. 'From Stettin in the Baltic to Trieste in the Adriatic, an Iron Curtain has descended across the Continent,' he declaimed. Aware of his intentions beforehand, both Truman and Attlee were worried his remarks would worsen international tensions with Stalin, but the fact Churchill addressed a crowd of 40,000 in a town whose population amounted to 7,000 was evidence his speech had been heavily promoted beforehand, with press releases scattered like confetti, in order for every conceivable news outlet to report each syllable. The widespread international reporting of the 'Iron Curtain' words was as remarkable as the phrase itself, which eventually became shorthand for the entire Cold War.

It was on Attlee's watch when the great victory parade of 6 June 1946 took place in London. Over four miles long, it included more than 500 vehicles from the armed services, and a fly-past of 300 aircraft. Overseas contingents also marched, including personnel from Belgium, Brazil, China, Czechoslovakia, France, Greece, Luxembourg, the Netherlands and the United States. Not, however, Poland. Attlee's government were still in thrall to the socialist ideals of the Soviets (his MPs had sung 'The Red Flag' on the assembly of the new Parliament on 1 August 1945), and requested a party of pro-Stalin Polish personnel from Warsaw. They did not invite any of the numerous Free Polish forces exiled to the

United Kingdom, who had fought for Britain and themselves so well in the air, at sea and on land.

Churchill led the protests at their exclusion, the result of Foreign Office advice not to offend Stalin. An insultingly last-minute concession, an invitation to the march of twenty-five Free Polish Battle of Britain pilots, was turned down. Their threatened presence caused the Warsaw Poles to pull out, as did deputations from the Soviet Union and Yugoslavia. It was an unnecessary insult, a shoddy episode still remembered by Poles today, but would not have happened had Winston been supervising this celebration of victory, as he did in 1919.

Churchill continued to concentrate mainly on international affairs and, later in 1946, at Zurich on 19 September, with great prescience and ahead of the sympathies of most, he announced: 'The first step in the recreation of the European family must be a partnership between France and Germany... [and] to form a Council of Europe.' The Zurich speech was as important as his 'Iron Curtain' one. To avoid any repeat of tragedy on the Continent, he essentially pleaded for a United States of Europe, but in which Britain would assist, but not be a part.

Five years later, the average Briton had become disillusioned with Attlee's domestic administration, which had also committed conscript servicemen to fighting unpopular wars in Malaya from June 1948 and Korea in August 1950. Having learned a lesson from his confrontational 'Gestapo speech' of 1945, and trading on slogans such as 'If you destroy a free market, you create a black market', and 'The nationalisation of industry is the doom of trade unionism',

Churchill returned to office after the 25 October 1951 general election. His regaining the keys to Downing Street was less the nation's desire for their wartime leader's comeback (though this undoubtedly played a part) and more a judgement that Labour's policies and politicians, technically in office since May 1940, were stale and exhausted. The deaths of several key figures; continuing austerity and increased rationing of the wartime kind (sales of bacon, bread, flour, potatoes, clothing, meat, sugar and coal were all restricted into the 1950s); the prolongation of conscription; and the shrinking of empire, as a source of raw materials and as an overseas market, all contributed to disenchantment with Attlee's version of socialism and a desire to give the Tories another chance. Significant, too, was the removal by the Conservative Research Department (headed by Butler) of the blimpish image of the old party.

Churchill determined Britain needed 'several years of quiet, steady administration', which is exactly what it got. His touch was light: there was no effort to unpick any innovations of the Attlee administration, and Churchill's Liberal instincts steered his second premiership towards a Disraeli-type 'one-nation' conservatism, leaving control of most domestic affairs to his Chancellor, Butler. While Churchill's wartime Chancellor, Kingsley Wood (1881–1943), had argued the extension of state intervention and significant expense envisioned by Beveridge would be 'an impracticable financial commitment', it had proven to be the main driver behind the 1945 general election with its social consensus to build a 'New Jerusalem', a Britain fit for those who had endured wartime hardship and sacrifice, both at home and on the front line. If expensive, the generous social policies which emerged after 1945, not least the creation of the National Health Service, but also an extensive council house-building programme, extended educational provision and enhanced welfare benefits, price controls and pensions, were central to Britain's post-war reconstruction and a sense of moving on from the hardship of the 'hungry thirties', when poverty was widespread and state support was limited.

The newly returned Prime Minister soon demonstrated he had lost none of his wartime energy, sitting down to an early breakfast, rounded off with a whisky and soda and the inevitable cigar, after a mammoth twenty-one-hour debate in the Commons, aged seventy-six. Yet his second premiership was marred by distress at Britain and the United States growing apart, despite the arrival of his old wartime friend and D-Day commander, Dwight Eisenhower, at the White House in January 1953.

With Churchill chasing opportunities to host world summits (a term he himself had coined), particularly after the death of Stalin in March 1953, the main obsession of Tory parliamentarians became his retirement date. Meanwhile, Churchill made three formal trips to the United States in 1952–54, on the last one receiving a note from President Eisenhower: 'Dear Winston... Am desirous that you stay with me... at the White House.' It was a conscious reprise of the warm relationship between Roosevelt and Winston, and of the latter's wartime visit to the White House of December 1941.

In 1953 Churchill was also awarded the Nobel Prize in Literature. He had expected the Peace Prize, for which he was twice nominated in 1945 and 1950, but had been a nominee for the literature prize in most years since 1946. According to his private secretary Anthony Montague Browne, Winston was disappointed it wasn't the Peace Prize, for he 'deeply wished to be remembered as a peacemaker'. In the year of his award, he was up against the stiff competition of thirteen others, including Walter de la Mare, Graham Greene, Robert Frost and Ernest Hemingway. The paperwork cited his 'his mastery of historical and biographical description as well as... brilliant oratory in defending exalted human values', meaning it was his rousing wartime speeches which tipped the balance in his favour: an interesting interpretation of 'literature'. He was unwell at the time of the award that December, and so Clemmie and Mary flew to Stockholm to collect it on his behalf.

The coronation of Queen Elizabeth II (2 June 1953) and his own eightieth birthday (30 November 1954) provided opportunities to retire, but the various illnesses of his designated heir, Eden, conspired to keep Churchill in office. Winston's valet, Norman McGowan, remembered a train journey from this era when his master, head out of the window to get a better view, was suddenly hauled back inside by his detective. Said McGowan of the Prime Minister's near-decapitation: 'My guv'nor smiled and observed, "Anthony Eden nearly got himself a new job then, didn't he?"' Churchill had suffered a hernia in June 1947, and two strokes in August 1949 and June 1953 (another would follow in October 1956), but it was Clemmie who gently persuaded her husband to quit on 5 April 1955. Like her father, Elizabeth II offered a dukedom (this time of London), which was again declined, but he had in 1953 accepted from her the highest degree of knighthood, also offered by her father but refused in 1945, the Garter, bringing more initials (this time KG) to the jumbled alphabet which already followed his name.

After KG, the spines of his later books indicated Winston was also OM (a member of the Order of Merit, awarded in 1946), CH (a Companion of Honour, bestowed in 1922) and PC (a Privy Counsellor of both the United Kingdom, appointed in 1907, and, from 1941, Canada). After this distinguished quartet, publishers drew the line, though Churchill's entries in *Who's Who* also identified he held the TD (Territorial Decoration, acknowledging his long service in the reserve forces); and was an FRS (Fellow of the Royal Society, bestowed in 1941), an RA (Royal Academician, awarded in 1948 for his many paintings) and a DL (Deputy Lieutenant of Kent, appointed in 1949).

Alive to his image, the knighthood did not affect the 'Winston Churchill' brand – it was merely preceded by 'Sir'. In November 1958, de Gaulle bestowed the *Croix de la Libération* on the Briton. At a ceremony in Paris, the French leader declaimed: 'I want Sir Winston to know this. Today's ceremony means France remembers what she owes him. I want him to know this: the man who has just had the honour of bestowing this distinction upon him values and admires him more than ever.' It was a highly charged moment which left both old warriors beyond wet-eyed. Valet McGowan remembered warning Winston his *Médaille Militaire* ribbon should be fixed to his left lapel. Churchill ignored him. 'It is worn on the right,' he insisted. Before the reception was over, all the attendees had changed theirs to the wrong lapel also. Sheepishly, the former Prime Minister concluded: 'The French are the best diplomats in the world.'

In 1959, Eisenhower invited Churchill for his last visit to the White House. Ike and Winston were both keen students of the American Civil War and the thirty-fourth President recalled the Briton had once written a chapter of alternative history, 'If Lee Had Not Won the Battle of Gettysburg' (the most prominent essay in the multi-authored collection *If It Had Happened Otherwise*, published in 1931).* Accordingly, he arranged for an aerial tour of the battlefield, adjacent to the presidential family retreat, by the novel method of helicopter. The President's son John noted how the years and several strokes had taken their toll on Britain's bulldog, but the decline in Winston's final decade was slow and enabled the world to shower more honours on the fading knight. He was too ill to cross the Atlantic again, this time for the award of honorary US citizenship by John F. Kennedy on 9 April 1963. The thirty-fifth American President, seven months away from his assassin's bullet, was probably the only world leader to be able to outmatch Winston's wordsmithery:

> Whenever and wherever tyranny threatened, he has always championed liberty. Facing firmly toward the future, he has never forgotten the past. Serving six monarchs of his native Great Britain, he has served all men's freedom and dignity. In the dark days and darker nights

---

* Churchill's essay was an exercise in 'double' counterfactual history, in which an imagined historian from a world in which Confederate general Robert E. Lee won the Battle of Gettysburg tries to imagine a future in which he did not.

when Britain stood alone, and most men save Englishmen
despaired of England's life, he mobilized the English language and sent it into battle... A child of the House of
Commons, he became in time its father... No statement or
proclamation can enrich his name. The name Sir Winston
Churchill is already legend.

Churchill's response, read out by his son, Randolph, was
nothing like as eloquent.

Relinquishing his parliamentary constituency of Woodford
only at the 15 October 1964 general election, which ended
Labour's thirteen years in opposition and ushered in the
young Harold Wilson, the former premier suffered a severe
stroke on 15 January of the following year, to the surprise
of few. Much of the globe paused on news of his death nine
days later.

Plans for Winston's send-off, Operation Hope Not,
drawn up from 1953 by the subject himself, were constantly
revised, mainly because 'the pall-bearers kept dying', as
one of his wartime commanders, Lord Louis Mountbatten,
explained. Over 300,000 filed past his coffin as it lay in
state in Westminster Hall for three days (the long queue is
this author's first memory) and a state funeral at St Paul's
Cathedral followed on 30 January. The great weight of his
lead-lined oaken coffin was borne by eight men from the 2nd
Grenadier Guards, whose predecessors he had commanded
in 1916. One of them, twenty-five-year-old Lance Sergeant
Lincoln Perkins, later remembered whispering to his charge
throughout the procession: 'Don't worry, sir, we'll look after
you.' Pall-bearers included Churchill's successor, by then the

Earl Attlee, at eighty-two so frail he had to remain seated in the freezing January cold, having exhausted himself at the previous day's rehearsal, but determined to pay last respects to his wartime chief. Ironically it was Attlee the socialist who took the peerage, whereas Churchill, grandson of a duke, twice refused his.

Attended by fifty heads of state and representatives from sixty-two other nations, the occasion would be the last BBC commentary by the first of Britain's great broadcast journalists, Richard Dimbleby, who had made his name reporting on both of Churchill's premierships and would die from cancer within the year. Hyde Park echoed to a ninety-gun salute, one shot for each year of Churchill's long life. Then Britain's greatest knight was placed on a gun carriage draped with the Union flag, on which rested his thirty-seven orders, decorations and medals received between 1885 and 1963. They included twenty awarded by Great Britain, three by France, two each by Belgium, Denmark, Luxembourg and Spain, and one each by Egypt, Libya, Nepal, the Netherlands, Norway and the United States.

Resembling in every respect a royal funeral, the carriage was drawn by ninety-eight sailors, with forty more behind holding drag ropes, and included nine military bands and eighteen army regiments, competing with an overflight of RAF Lightning jets. Yet it was the sight of London's dockyard crane jibs being lowered as the motor vessel *Havengore* proceeded along the Thames with the catafalque which provoked the most tears on a wet-eyed day, as had his words in 1940.

His slow riverine exit was a tribute to all Churchill's associations with matters nautical, from his time at the Admiralty to his roles as Lord Warden of the Cinque Ports (his wartime code name was 'Colonel Warden'), Elder Brother of Trinity House (responsible for the nation's lighthouses) and Member of the Royal Yacht Squadron, each office requiring a splendid uniform. The man who had crammed so many lives into one was borne to Waterloo station (a detail he insisted on, knowing protocol would demand de Gaulle's presence at the railway terminus named after Wellington's great victory), and conveyed by special train to Oxfordshire. Tens, some say hundreds, of thousands stood by the trackside in reverence as the Battle of Britain-class steam locomotive *Winston Churchill*, Pullman car *Lydia* (formerly part of his wartime command train), special hearse van and four other carriages passed. Charles de Gaulle's magnanimous note of condolence to Her Majesty the Queen read: 'In the great drama, he was the greatest of all.'

Responses to Churchill have been as wide as the oceans. On one hand, the Churchill allure failed for the professional contrarian and novelist Evelyn Waugh. 'Rallied the nation indeed!' he opined a mere seventy-two hours after Winston's death. 'How we despised his orations.' Aneurin 'Nye' Bevan, Attlee's Minister of Health, warmed to this theme, contending he 'did not think Churchill was the lion's roar of Britain in the war', while historian A. J. P. Taylor argued: 'Churchill had no vision for the future, only a tenacious defence of the past.' Yet none of this sniping gets near the subject of their acerbity. Historian R. W. Thompson thought: 'For Churchill, it was never England right or wrong, but simply England.' His great wartime deputy, dyed-in-the-wool socialist and Prime Ministerial successor had the decency to muse: 'By any reckoning Winston Churchill was one of the greatest men that history records... Energy and poetry in my view really sums him up... History set him the job that he was the ideal man to do,' while Sir George Mallaby, Cabinet Office Undersecretary during the war, recorded: '[Churchill] was free with abuse and complaint... exacting beyond reason and ruthlessly critical... Not only did he get away with it but nobody really wanted him otherwise. He was unusual, unpredictable, exciting, original, stimulating, provocative, outrageous, uniquely experienced, abundantly talented, humorous, entertaining... a great man.'

Sir Winston Leonard Spencer Churchill was buried in a surprisingly unostentatious, though still much-visited grave next to his parents in Bladon, the estate village of his kins-men, the dukes of Marlborough. He was joined twelve years later, in 1977, by his beloved Clemmie, who by then had become Baroness Spencer-Churchill, the gift of a grateful nation for supporting her husband. The life peerage was a typical suggestion of Attlee's, who had become a close per-sonal friend. He wished to grant Churchill's widow a title which would outrank the Soviet Order of the Red Banner, bestowed for Clemmie's fundraising efforts by Winston's war-time ally, Russia. It was granted by the new Prime Minister, Harold Wilson, who had worked for Beveridge during the war, on 17 May 1965. Formidable to the last, after her hus-band's passing, it was discovered she had connived in the destruction of a large portrait of Churchill, the gift of both Houses of Parliament on his eightieth birthday. Painted by the modernist Graham Sutherland, neither she nor Winston had cared for it.

Winston's passing kept the world's journalists busy for weeks. 'Hommage à un Géant' (tribute to a giant), read the front page of France's illustrated weekly *Paris Match* on 30 January 1965. Like most newspapers and magazines of the moment, it noted not just the Briton's death, but the end of the imperial era into which he was born and which he had come to represent. Immediately, the Royal Mint elevated Winston to the near-status of Roman emperor, in issuing 19.6 million 'Churchill crowns' (then worth five shillings, or a quarter of a pound), the first British coin to depict a non-royal personage.

Future writers may demonise or deify him, but if any single Prime Minister has ever found the heart of the British nation and understood what makes it tick, particularly in times of adversity, it was Winston Churchill. Writing at this distance in time, it is difficult to appreciate the devotion most of Britain's senior decision-makers had for him. Let the by no means uncritical Field Marshal Alan Brooke, who conferred with his political master nearly every day during the war, speak for them all:

> I shall always look back on the years I worked with him as some of the most difficult and trying ones of my life. For all that, I thank God that I was given an opportunity of working alongside of such a man, and of having my eyes opened to the fact that occasionally such supermen exist on this earth.

After nearly sixty-five years, the correspondent of the *Church Family Newspaper* had proven more prophetically accurate than he could possibly have imagined. Winston Churchill did climb very high up the ladder of life. The world needed such a man. He made history, influenced men's minds, carried conviction because he was in earnest; and the English-speaking peoples were proud, and remain proud to call Winston Churchill one of their own.

FURTHER READING AND
ACKNOWLEDGEMENTS

This has been a necessarily brief gallop through Winston Churchill's exhaustively long and full life in the 150th year of his birth, and I hear you thirsting for more. In terms of recent scholarship and secondary sources, Allen Packwood's *Cambridge Companion to Winston Churchill* (2023) offers nineteen chapters by different authors on where we are today. For my money, the best three full biographies are by Andrew Roberts (*Churchill: Walking with Destiny*, 2018), Roy Jenkins (*Churchill*, 2001) and Martin Gilbert (*Churchill: A Life*, 1991, a condensed version of his eight volumes). Roberts also penned the terrific biography of our subject's 1940 rival for power, Lord Halifax, in *The Holy Fox* (1991). I have always appreciated Robert Rhodes James's aged but still useful analysis of Winston's pre-1940 life, *Churchill: A Study in Failure, 1900–1939*, published in 1970. In terms of Winston as a scribe, David Reynolds's *In Command of History: Churchill Fighting and Writing the Second World War* (2004) is a key read. For

Winston's family, Sonia Purnell's *First Lady: The Life and Wars of Clementine Churchill* (2015), John and Celia Lee's *Winston and Jack: The Churchill Brothers* (2007) and Mary Soames's *A Daughter's Tale* (2011) are important sources. Randolph's sad tale is told in Josh Ireland's *Churchill & Son* (2021). Purnell also penned an incisive biography of daughter-in-law Pamela, in *Kingmaker: Pamela Churchill Harriman's Astonishing Life of Seduction, Intrigue and Power* (2024). Well worth your time is Robin Prior's comparative history of Britain in the two world wars, *Conquer We Must: A Military History of Britain, 1914–1945* (2022). Winston's military life is covered by Con Coughlin's *Churchill's First War* (2013) and Richard Holmes's *In the Footsteps of Churchill* (2005), while Barry Gough penned the very readable *Churchill and Fisher: Titans at the Admiralty* (2017). Andrew Lownie's *Traitor King* (2022) offers an uncompromising view of Edward VIII, later the Duke of Windsor.

Other important sources include Sir John Colville's 1985 insight into working for Chamberlain, Churchill and Attlee in *The Fringes of Power: Downing Street Diaries 1939–1955*, while the life of Admiral Jackie Fisher is well explored in *Fisher's Face* by Jan Morris (1995). Richard Toye edited an important collection of fourteen essays in *Winston Churchill: Politics, Strategy and Statecraft* (2017); Tim Bouverie's *Appeasement: Chamberlain, Hitler, Churchill and the Road to War* (2019) is the latest word on this policy of the 1930s, whilst the first, *Guilty Men* by 'Cato' (the journalists Michael Foot, Frank Owen and Peter Howard), was reissued by Penguin to mark its sixtieth anniversary of publication, in 2000.

On his art, Paul Rafferty's *Winston Churchill: Painting on the French Riviera* (2020) will do you well, as will Richard Toye's study of his oratory, *The Roar of the Lion: The Untold Story of Churchill's World War II Speeches* (2013). Toye also published the authoritative *Lloyd George and Churchill* (2007). Andrew Chatterton's discovery of Britain's resistance movements can be found in Britain's *Secret Defences* (2022); Bundeswehr historian Karl-Heinz Frieser's *The Blitzkrieg Legend: The 1940 Campaign in the West* (2005) remains the best explanation for the fall of France; Erik Larson's story of Winston in the Blitz, *The Splendid and the Vile* (2020) offers a page-turning account of 1940, also covered in John Lukacs's magisterial *Five Days in London: May 1940* (1999), while David Lough treats us to an innovative study of Winston's finances in *No More Champagne: Churchill and His Money* (2015). For spiritual matters, *God and Churchill* (2015) by Jonathan Sandys and Wallace Henley offers insight, while Cita Stelzer's *Working with Winston* (2019) introduces us to those supporting the great man in his many lives. His principal military subordinates are detailed in John Keegan's unsurpassed *Churchill's Generals* (1991), chief among them Brooke, whose own *War Diaries 1939–1945* (edited by Alex Danchev and Daniel Todman) appeared in 2002, and Ismay, whose biography, *General Hastings 'Pug' Ismay: Soldier, Statesman, Diplomat*, by John Kiszely, was published in 2024. The aforementioned Richard Holmes covered Winston's homes and headquarters with *Churchill's Bunker: The Secret Headquarters at the Heart of Britain's Victory* (2009). Chartwell was key to Winston's life, about which much of Sarah Gristwood and Margaret Gaskin's *Churchill: An Extraordinary Life* (2019) revolves.

For Winston's post-war world, Anthony Tucker-Jones's *Churchill: Cold War Warrior* (2024) is a favourite, while Robert Blake and William Roger Louis's *Churchill: A Major New Reassessment of His Life in Peace and War* (1993) contains an edited collection of twenty-nine useful essays by various scholars. Well, what about Winston and Ireland, or the decline of Empire? Can we have more on his relationship with organised labour before the Great War, or with General Montgomery, the sacrifice of the Highland Division in 1940, Zionism and the wider Middle East, India, poison gas, atomic weapons, his family and friends, 1951–55 administration, Russia or the United States, I hear you ask? Obviously in a book of this length, there are omissions. Treat this as an introduction, balanced to give you a flavour of this complex and fascinating individual.

I am most grateful to my boon companion, Tim Loughton, for his stirring foreword; to Mr and Mrs Ed Haislmaier for the loan of their various châteaux in which to compose this work; to Katherine Carter, curator of Chartwell, Andy Chatterton, historian of the Auxiliary Units, Churchill scholars Lord (Andrew) Roberts and Sonia Purnell for their helpful observations; Paul Beaver assisted me with his knowledge of Pol Roger champagne, and Major General Alastair Bruce of Crionaich on matters of protocol. To Mr Brad Pitt and Ms Angela Jolie, for allowing me to view their artwork, *Tower of the Koutoubia Mosque*, which has since been sold at auction for £8.3 million. Also to the *Church Family Newspaper* (now the *Church Times*), for the unlikely find of their 16 November

1900 edition with its prophetic account of young Winston Churchill's London lecture (actually given on 30 October), the first time it has resurfaced since then. With every book, I like to tip my hat to my friend, colleague and mentor, the late Professor Richard Holmes, who enriched my journey as a young historian. My agent, Patrick Walsh, editors Karen Farrington and Alex Middleton, publicist Ruth Killick, designer Alex Billington, and publisher Mark Richards at Swift Press have ensured the smoothest of rides from inception to print. I hold my hand up to any errors, but after a year of immersion in Churchilliana, I am still amazed at the fullness of his life, flaws and all, but chiefly its warmth and splendour.

PETER CADDICK-ADAMS, 2024